THE SOCIAL HUMANISM OF CALVIN

THE
SOCIAL
HUMANISM
OF
Calvin

André Biéler

Translated by Paul T. Fuhrmann
Foreword by W. A. Visser't Hooft

JOHN KNOX PRESS
Richmond, Virginia

A translation of *L'humanisme social de Calvin* by André Biéler, published in 1961 by Éditions Labor et Fides, Geneva.

The Scripture renderings in this book are Calvin's.

The translation of Calvin's passages is our own.

Library of Congress Catalog Card Number: 64-11878

© M. E. Bratcher 1964

Printed in the United States of America

9590(20)6039

CONTENTS

FOREWORD

A man can speak simply and clearly only of things which he knows well. After giving us a profound and original analysis of the social ethics of Calvin (in a large and fully documented volume entitled *The Economic and Social Thought of Calvin**), Dr. Biéler now offers us this remarkably clear summary of the central convictions which dominate the ethics of the Genevese Reformer.

Many a reader will be astonished at meeting in these pages a Calvin who is quite different from the current image of him. How could Calvin, the reader will ask, be a humanist caring for the restoration of the human person? Was he not obsessed by the glory of God? How could Calvin possibly be a social personalist interested in social problems? Is he not known to us as the father of *laissez-faire* capitalism? How could Calvin in many respects be a defender of equality? Were we not taught that he was an autocrat? Yet our author, Pastor Biéler, knows what he is talking about. Those readers who doubt some of Dr. Biéler's statements may look at his main and much larger work mentioned above— *La pensée économique et sociale de Calvin*. The reader will find there innumerable quotations and references to Calvin's many volumes as well as the Bible references and passages which Calvin expounded or had in mind.

The sad truth is that Calvin has too often been seen through Calvinism and Puritanism, which are later outlooks. These have made a selection in Calvin's legacy of ideas and left aside important aspects of our Reformer's thought. Besides leaving aside many of Calvin's ideas, the later Calvinistic churches moreover

---

* *La pensée économique et sociale de Calvin,* published in Geneva for her University by Georg & Co. in 1961.

did not for long maintain the courage and vitality necessary for the accomplishment of the prophetic mission entrusted to them— a mission which, for Calvin, had been an essential duty of the church.

If men had paid attention to Calvin, certain great misfortunes would never have happened. I will offer one example. Everybody now knows the immense importance which the slogan "To each according to his needs, from each according to his capacities" has had for Communism. Lenin thought that Communism would reach its final goal the day this slogan had become a reality. Lenin said that this slogan came from Marx. And Marx had really used it. But neither Lenin nor Marx was aware that three hundred years before Marx, Calvin had already formulated this thought in his exposition of II Corinthians 8:13-14. Calvin had there said: "God wills that there be proportion and equality among us, that is, each man is to provide for the needy according to the extent of his means so that no man has too much and no man has too little." If the churches had really taken seriously and practiced this teaching, Communists could never have been enabled to take this basically biblical thought out of its Christian context and transplant it into their materialistic and totalitarian outlook.

Confronted as we are today with a disoriented society where the awareness of human solidarity and the sense of social responsibility are ever becoming weaker, the time has come to reconsider and set forth Calvin's teaching about Christian humanism. The humanism of Calvin is founded on the humanism of God and demands a society wherein man acts as a creature responsible before God and responsible for his brethren.

W. A. Visser't Hooft

I

THE PERSON AND SOCIETY

There are strange similarities between the sixteenth century and our time.

One of them is that the most outstanding thinkers of today radically question man.

The upsetting of all order which followed the Renaissance and the discovery of the New World had led men of that time to ask with anguish, "What is the nature of man?" The Protestant Reformation has not only been a rediscovery of God. It has also given a decisive answer to the question: "Who is man?"

Today we are at a similar crossroad. Modern scientific discoveries as well as the tragic events (which for twenty years have stained mankind with blood and caused a whole train of indescribable cruelties) have not only shaken traditional ways of thinking but have forced every thinking man (be he a man in the street or a scholar) to ask himself, "Who is this strange being called man? Where does he come from and where does he go? In what way can man know himself with certainty?"

These questions are really one. And it fills us with anguish because we feel that in this life we can do no good unless we first have satisfactorily answered that question. If I do not know who I am, no love is possible; man and woman seek one another without ever meeting; work becomes dull; society cannot be built; there is no hope anywhere.

Now, this preliminary question remains unanswered for the great masses of men in our time; and the anguish of men becomes worse as they realize that the answers given to them are deceitful. As a matter of fact, some persons want us to believe that today there are only two groups of men: the atheists, on one side, and

9

believers in God, on the other. Is it worth while to sacrifice our life for either group? Indeed it does not take very long to discover that atheism is found everywhere: a dogmatic atheism, on the one side, and a pragmatic atheism, on the other—both lead ultimately to the same delusion and the same betrayal of man. Through various roads of intuition or reflection, all men little by little fall into the same pessimism, into the same spiritual nihilism which is highly proclaimed for millions of silent men by such writers as Albert Camus, Jean Paul Sartre, Jean Anouilh, and, in an easier fashion, Françoise Sagan.

By his stubborn rejection of outworn conventional values, Camus has truly accomplished an intellectually and spiritually healthful operation on our weary Western world. Is it not a great merit indeed to lay bare the equivocal mixture of political ideology and religious idealism which in most of our Christian churches still passes under the name of Christianity and takes the place of Christianity? But are the writers we have named offering anything constructive? They all end with a pessimistic denial of man and with a philosophy of the absurd which urges us even more to rediscover a new humanism. Before any discussion and action in the present world, it is important to find out what man is. No personal ethics or political theory can be elaborated unless this preliminary question is answered.

Now, the humanism of John Calvin is found in the Gospels and its essence has lost none of its value for today.

But before entering the social problems of wealth and work, let us here examine briefly the nature of the human person and society.

1. The Foundations of the Humanism of Calvin

At the beginning of their impatient search for the true nature of man, the humanists and Reformers had made a common cause against traditional Christendom. The church of that time had undergone the same change as has the conventional Christianity of our day. Taking itself as its own end, it had imprisoned man in religion instead of freeing him from religion and opening him to Christ.

Together then, humanists and Reformers were in quest of true man—of man freed of all false mysticisms and social servitudes which had for so long denatured him, that is, altered man's essential qualities. But soon humanists and Reformers parted ways. Some humanists were the heirs of pagan antiquity, the popularity of which the Italian Renaissance had restored. These men admired what makes up the external charm of man: man's art, man's culture, and man's social behavior, which for Machiavelli is politeness as well as political ability. This image of man was sufficient for these humanists, and they thought to find an answer (to their question about the destiny of man) nowhere except in man himself and in nature to which man belongs.

But other humanists were rather theological-minded and heirs of the most authentic elements of the Christian tradition. These men refused to accept such a simplification and abstraction of man. For them, true man could be rediscovered only by starting from God who alone can tell man who man is. With a vehemence which caused lively debates, they rejected the pretensions of those humanists who sought to know man by starting only from man.

In France, however, the intellectual climate was different. French humanism was more respectful of theology. The return to antiquity which the Renaissance sponsored was for a Lefèvre d'Etaples, a Marguerite of Navarre or a Guillaume Budé, and even for a François Rabelais, also a return to the springs of Jewish and Christian civilization. Hence these men studied anew the texts of the Old and New Testaments.

We must also say that under the clear sky of France the quest for God was less mystical than in the fogs of Germany. The French sought the living God not so much in the soul of Christian man as in God's Word, in the actual revelation of the Word given by God through his Holy Spirit who enlightens the ancient testimony of the prophets and apostles. The Godcenteredness of the French Reformers, however, did not dramatically exclude the mancenteredness of the humanists. Indeed the Christian thinkers in France insisted that both methods (the mancentered and the Godcentered) could contribute something to the knowledge of man.

This great French clearness in seeing differences of thought explains the extreme liberty taken by Calvin in combining the fascinating findings of humanism with the irreplaceable teachings of theology. Calvin did not fall into such deceptive syntheses as those which Roman Catholic scholasticism had attempted. At all costs Calvin avoided this dangerous and fearful temptation which, by the way, explains the vehement diatribes of a Luther against the confusions of an Erasmus.

Calvin was a humanist of the highest degree. He knew indeed how to add without confusion the revealed knowledge of man (which God discloses to his creature through Christ) to the natural self-knowledge (which man has by himself and which the humanists possessed).

For Calvin it was a question not so much of turning one's back on humanism as of going beyond and giving new dimensions to humanism. Calvin passed from a purely mancentered knowledge of man to a complete knowledge of man with the mystery of God at its center. At times and rather violently, Calvin opposed the humanists; however, he opposed not so much humanism itself as the atheism or exclusive mancenteredness of certain humanists. Calvin thought that intellectual pride limited these men and that their boundless confidence in man was incompatible with the Christian faith.

Let us now gather up our findings. The sum of medieval knowledge was theology—the study of God. The sum of the knowledge of the Renaissance was humanism—the study and knowledge of humanness. Now, the science of Calvin is a theological and social humanism which includes a study of man and society through a twofold knowledge of man by man, on the one hand, and a knowledge of man through God, on the other.

Who is man according to the humanism of Calvin? What man am I according to the thought of Calvin? These questions we must now answer.

2. *The Nature of Man*

Calvin does not think it realistic to question man, such as he is today, in order to find his true nature. In his present state man is in no position to say anything certain about himself. In fact man has kept only a dim and confused image of authentic human nature. Man is no longer the man he once was. Man no longer corresponds to his original stature. Sin has changed his nature. What can man know about man? Man can no longer know anything essential about himself. Certainly man's reason is still able to penetrate certain mysteries of his own secular nature and of his physical constitution and social mechanisms. Calvin has strongly insisted that in a certain measure human knowledge is adequate in the physical, intellectual, and even political fields. Thus Calvin has made great contributions toward assuring the development of modern sciences. This is evident from the numerical predominance of Protestant scientists in the Western world during the centuries which followed Calvin.

According to Calvin, however, human reason is unable to yield a deeper and more essential knowledge of man and society. Only God can communicate to man the ultimate identity of human nature. The reason is that the natural communication of man with God is broken. There is no way going from man to God. It is at this juncture that we meet the so-called radical pessimism of Calvin which is in reality his basic evangelicalism. Man by himself cannot find God again. Only God can communicate God to his creatures.

And God exercises this power. How? By addressing his Word to man and by sending his only Son who is God's eternal Word. This Son was an irruption in the midst of humanity at the time of Pontius Pilate, but the Son pre-existed from all eternity with God. To him the prophets as well as the apostles have rendered a clear testimony in the world both before and after his coming.

Now, what is this Word of God saying to man about man?

God's Word offers five successive aspects of man:

First, it tells man that since the beginning man was in the purpose of God. It tells what the original nature of man is.

Secondly, it shows what man is now in his actual humanness and in relation to his primordial nature.

Thirdly, it describes how God goes about restoring humanness into the humanness of his son Jesus Christ.

Fourthly, the Word teaches man what fallen man becomes on earth when man lets God take him in hand and benefit him with the restoration of humanness in Christ.

Finally, the Word teaches what man will be in the perfect world of God and what man will become at the end of time when he will have fully recovered his new nature.

What was man originally?

The Word of God gives an extremely pleasing picture of the primordial nature of man. It discloses an image of man such as no humanist ever had dared to conceive.

Man is indeed created in the image of God. "Man is the noblest and most excellent masterpiece," Calvin writes, "wherein the justice, wisdom, and goodness of God show forth." Moreover, man is placed at the center and at the head of all creation, and creation is destined to serve man. Man is "like a lieutenant of God in governing the world," Calvin says. Man's vocation imposes upon him the duty to explore and to subject all the resources of this vast universe. We shall later see the importance of this vocation from the point of view of economics.

In all this, however, man is man only if he remains himself subject to his Creator. Man is free only when he is a servant of God. Man enjoys authentic freedom only if he participates in the liberty of God. And he participates in God's freedom only by remaining subject to God. Outside this liberty received in subjection through love without constraint, there is nothing but slavery and self-annihilation. Man loses his liberty as soon as he, in seeking himself and a freedom of his own, turns away from God who is liberty. Man falls then into slavery to the world, to himself, and to nature. And man calls this slavery "his freedom"!

Such is the present situation of man.

By seeking to choose liberty outside of God, man has fallen. Yes, each day man falls into slavery. Man is a slave of himself, and his autonomy means his self-destruction. Man therefore walks toward death, and death is the end of every modern man.

The man whom we moderns know—the man whom we analyze, the man of psychology, the man whom science examines, the man of literature, and the man of profane humanism—is not the authentic man. He is only a pale shadow, a counterfeit, a caricature of man. This man has no hope whatever of reaching anything. In spite of his marvelous gifts which still witness in him to the majesty of the work of God, everything that the man of today undertakes is devoted to death and ends in death.

The desperate analysis of man so lucidly given by the Camus of any period is more just, more realistic, and more evangelical than the analysis given by religious and profane idealists. Although not intending to do so, these idealists deceive natural man by having him believe that merely imagining what a man wishes to become actually changes him into what he wants to be!

A pessimistic outlook on man, however, is not the only view which Calvin drew from the Gospels. It is at this juncture that Reformed humanism absolutely differs from our contemporary humanism of the absurd and from atheism. Calvin is aware that another man was among men. This man was the man of a new creation, the new Adam, the eternal Christ, who, for a few years, became on earth the Jesus of history, the legal son of Joseph.

In Jesus Christ we are to find again the man of the beginning, the true man in the eyes of God, the perfect image of the Creator. He is indeed the son of Mary's bosom and under the care of Joseph, but he is at the same time the beloved Son of God in whom the divine power of the Holy Spirit is active.

In Jesus Christ, therefore, we meet again true man, man entirely free, man in full possession of humanness, because that man is entirely subjected to God, without constraint, by the only possible bond—free love.

Henceforth fallen man—the denatured man that we are, every human creature—is going to be able to find through this only perfect creature the road to human restoration.

Of whatever race he be, to whatever religion he belong, under whatever sky his abode be, a man is going to be able to recover his humanity by listening to Christ Jesus and following him.

By entering through repentance (and baptism) in contact and communion with the resurrected and invisible Christ, man receives a new nature. Man finds again his true character. We must say that if the man who gives himself to Christ already recovers this new nature in potentiality, his new being can at present yet be only partially perceived in reality. Through sanctification the new nature emerges each day in the life of a man but it remains veiled by sin until death. We shall know our fully and completely restored humanness only in the world to come. But at the present time and until death, the humanness of the believer finds itself in conflict with his inhumanness. The believer is a forgiven and justified sinner, and a regenerated sinner, yet until the end of his days a sinner still.

Such is the authentic nature of man. Such is man's real image, dramatic and dynamic, as Calvin rediscovered it in the Gospels.

3. The Dynamism of the Person

In order to regenerate the man of whom we have just spoken, the Holy Spirit every day engages him in a daily combat, in a discipline, and, let us add, even in a real asceticism.

Transformed by Christ, the new man is henceforth in daily struggle with himself and with all the world-forces which denature him. Grace is not a gift which renders man passive. On the contrary, in order to activate all human potentialities, grace sets in motion an overflowing activity in man. In order to master well those potentialities and to accomplish fully his humanness, that man must continuously struggle and combat his own inhumanness.

The reason is that if a man refuses to take notice of the will of God as it is expressed in the law of the New and Old Testaments, man deteriorates by himself. He becomes corrupt, adulterates his own humanness, and loses his liberty.

In order to remain human, a man must impose a rigorous discipline upon himself.

First of all is a spiritual discipline. Through prayer and rigorous, continuous, and personal appropriation of Sacred Scripture, a man is to find ever anew contact and communion with Jesus Christ. Through mastery of his thought, heart, and body, he expresses the hold which the Holy Spirit has upon his person. Through dynamism of action and control of his individual and social behavior, he outwardly witnesses his subjection to the active love of God.

Yet, may we say it again, this discipline is an asceticism in freedom, a constraint which man freely imposes upon himself in order to possess himself. After a man has renounced himself, Christ indeed places him in possession of himself.

And this dynamism of the Holy Spirit, this power of love acting in a man, necessarily urges him to meet his neighbor. Man cannot do without his neighbor unless he mutilates his own humanness.

Hence let us examine what the person is in relationship with others.

4. The Constitution of Society

What we have just said about the human person and his nature is not sufficient to characterize truly either the person or human nature. So far we have spoken of man as if he could exist by himself, as if he could be man in solitariness.

Now, evangelical humanism, that is, the humanism of Calvin, is primarily a social humanism.

It is such first of all because by nature man is truly man only in proportion to his living in company of other men. A man becomes an accomplished man only in relationship with other human beings. "God has created man," Calvin says, "so that man may be a creature of fellowship."

This natural companionship is first of all expressed in a couple (man and woman relationship) and then complemented in the family community. Companionship is completed in work and in the interplay of economic exchanges. Human fellowship is realized in relationships which flow from the division of labor wherein each person has been called by God to a particular and partial work which complements the work of others. The mutual exchange of goods and services is the concrete sign of the profound solidarity* which unites humanity.

Man is normally called to live in a set of relationships, the chief of which are the couple, the family, and the working union or corporation.

But, like man himself, this primitive social order has undergone very serious perturbations.

Thinking to save his liberty, man has separated himself from God, thereby not only destroying his individual self but also changing the nature of social relationships. Man has distorted social life and economic exchanges. Thinking to find his freedom outside of God, man in fact ends by foundering in a combination of slaveries. He becomes a slave of his own nature, of his sexual and emotional life, and of his work. He becomes the tyrant of his neighbor each time that he avoids being his neighbor's slave. All natural hierarchies are corrupted.

Married life, family life, and social life are altogether falsified by the forfeiture and fall of man.

Thus society as known to us, that society in which we tie and untie our marriages, in which we weave and unweave the social bonds of our work, that society in which politicians are ever busy, that very concrete yet elusive society which our sociologists analyze, after all is not a normal society. On the contrary, our society is disorganized and basically vitiated. Its true nature necessarily escapes our knowledge. Rousseau's idea that society corrupts men who yet are born good is not biblical. Society is

---

* Translator's note: The word "solidarity" is seldom found in English, but it is currently used abroad in law, philosophy, sociology, and theology by men who consider mankind as a "solid," that is, an organic unit, hence man as one solid ("solidary") with mankind. Since the time of Calvin, the fact of social solidarity gave birth to several theories whose common principle is based on the mere fact that because he is born in a society, the individual thereby benefits from all anterior social efforts and must in turn contribute to the common good. Solidarity means common dependence among men so that some cannot develop into persons and be happy if the others don't.

corrupt because individuals also are corrupt. Society as known to us is the deteriorated residuum of that original society which God has conceived, which he wants anew, and which today he pursues through his own method of restoration.

Now, how is such restoration possible?

We have just spoken of the new humanness which man receives through contact and communion with Christ. Now we must emphasize that man never receives this new nature by himself alone. By definition the birth into Christian life is a communal phenomenon. Individual Christian life does not exist. To believe that there is such a thing as individual life is a deception and a deceiving religious illusion. The reason is that contact and communion with Christ necessarily make any man or woman a member of Christ's body. Christ is the Head of this body. Each believer regenerated through faith is attached to this body. He becomes one of its indispensable members. The Christian life is therefore impossible outside the visible and coherent communion of the church. "God's elect," says Calvin, "are in Christ joined in such a way that they all depend on one Chief and Head, and are made one same body." Moreover, in spite of external divisions, the church herself, as well as her members, is in the whole world and at all times *one*. "The church," says our Reformer, "is called catholic or universal because in our opinion no two or three churches can be made without tearing Jesus Christ to pieces."

Certainly the church as an institution, the conventional church, is not always and necessarily the church of Jesus Christ. The church may easily become, and in history has often become, a sociological and religious organization which, although using the name of Christ, denies Christ in fact. But, inversely, there is no real Christian life outside a visible community, however numerically and humanly feeble it might be. "Because it can never happen," says Calvin, "that those who are truly persuaded that God is their common Father and that Christ is the only Chief and Head of them all, be not united among themselves in brotherly love to the end that they communicate together for their mutual progress."

Now the existence in the midst of society of this cell and

nucleus which is the community of Christians, however small it may be, constitutes the small priming for the social restoration of humanness. It is so, of course, if this community is truly Christian. The church community is the society of men and women who through Christ have been restored to their humanness. The church is the embryo of an entirely new world where the once perverted social relations find anew their original nature.

It is therefore in the church community, in the parish of re-generated Christians, that we men may rediscover an image of restored social life, of society such as God had willed it. In reality this image is always fragmentary because sin always survives in the life of each Christian. Nevertheless this image of a renewed society corresponds to the purpose of God. Thanks to the active presence of the living Christ, all the natural cells of our corrupt society may find in the church the wholesome life which God had conceived and purposed for them.

Let us consider first of all the couple, that is, man and woman. By giving them back their humanness, Christ makes it possible that man and woman find themselves again face to face. Only the daily intervention of Christ can restore the couple which by nature is divided. And Christ eliminates man's tendencies to consider woman as inferior. In Christ there is no longer man or woman. "There is no distinction between male and female," says Calvin. "With regard to the Kingdom of God, which is spiritual," he adds, "there is no difference between man and woman."

On the other hand, Christ gives to the unmarried the courage and joy to follow their vocation. In this disordered society where each person no longer finds his partner, celibacy restores a man or a woman who lives in faith. We mean that celibacy makes a single man or woman more an authentic person than would a marriage without communion with Christ.

Let us consider the family next. Only the mediation of Christ can reconstitute the family bonds which are so easily torn apart by the multiple forces of sin.

As for the other forms of society, there are various types of social relations. Communion in Jesus Christ abolishes or sur-mounts all sociological divisions which separate human beings and destroy the harmonious life of society. As we shall later see in detail, the same happens with work relations. In Christ there is no longer slave or free man. This means that Christians who live an authentic faith become aware of their social determinism. In other words, they realize that human action is not entirely free but is largely determined by external forces acting on the will. Conscious of that, authentic Christians rise above their natural environment and meet their brethren without any kind of discrimination.

The same is true with national relations. The diversity of national characters is social wealth and a resource to be cultivated. But nationalism (which extols these differences and makes them sacred and exclusive values) is a pernicious form of paganism. As nationalism vitiates human society, it is absolutely contrary and hostile to the Christian faith. In Christ there is no longer either Jew or Greek. This means that in the bosom of the universal communion of Christians all national antagonisms are abolished. A foreigner in the local Christian community is to be welcomed there as a brother.

In this connection we must recall the fierce war which Calvin waged against that perverted form of patriotism which is religious nationalism. Religious nationalism shows up each time that we set up our country as a sacred value and identify the cult of our ancestors or of our nation with Christian worship. The authenticity of a Christian church is to be tested in the light of her spiritual judgment in this matter. A church's rejection of all foggy confusion of church and nation is a mark of her authenticity.

It goes without saying that the abolition of divisions between races is a characteristic of all authentic Christian communities.

The restoration of social bonds in the church includes the relation between rich and poor. We shall later devote a special section to this problem. At present it is enough to indicate here that the spiritual fellowship which unites the members of the body of Christ (particularly at the moment of celebrating the Lord's Supper) is necessarily accompanied by a mutual communication or exchange of services and material goods between the members of that body. If this does not happen, the spiritual fellowship (which these individuals seek) is a pure religious illusion and a dangerous deception. "The saints," Calvin says, "are gathered into the society of Christ on condition that they mutually exchange among themselves the gifts conferred to them by God." Of this imperative need a strong and typically Calvinian organization was born in Calvin's church: the deaconship, which in Calvin's time was the organ for redistributing the church members' goods and services both within and outside the community.

Our present-day stewardship or deaconship is only a pale and poor remnant of this institution of Calvin's day. The awareness of being a member of the body of Christ and the sense of responsibility flowing from that awareness have practically disappeared in many of our churches.

We can see from these examples that the social humanism of Calvin not only seeks to restore the person in its original humanness but aims at renewing society in its various forms of existence.

5. Church, Society, and State

The restoration of society of which we have just spoken is the work of Christ within the community of believers and in the midst of the church. Now, the real church is never and nowhere to be confused with the whole of society. We find therefore beside the Christian communities an important margin of mankind which does not know that its restoration is possible. Moreover, the church herself is only partially restored on earth. Until the end of time the church remains a prisoner of disorder. Calvin thinks that if the world were left to itself, it would collapse in complete chaos. The advent of the church and the birth of a new humanity within the old humanity are not sufficient to resist the thrust of forces which destroy the person and society. The renewal brought by Christ meets strong resistance in the very heart of humanity. The church ought to witness to this renewal, but when it is a question of social problems the church of today is not yet aware of her missionary duty to penetrate the whole body of our present society.

To avoid everything's being swallowed up by chaos and disorder, God brought up within the whole of society a provisional order which Calvin calls the political order.

This order does not consist in Christ's renewing man unto liberty but, on the contrary, in external constraint which maintains man in a relative morality.

The agents of this order are, on the one hand, external and conventional moral law governing individuals and, on the other hand, state law enforced through governmental institutions.

This political order is relative, that is to say, it is a transitory order in the expectation of the end of time. Only after the Last Judgment will mankind fully find its original nature. Men will then spontaneously live in social peace because men will freely be subjected to God's order. While waiting for this final consummation, and in order to live, all societies need a provisory order, that is, a human system which is the political order.

This political order is not without relation to God's order. In any society, the political order must indeed represent, as nearly as possible, the order of God, while yet keeping present the spiritual development of people in a given place and at a given time.

The more faithful Christians are, the more numerous they will be in society and the better the political order will be.

Conversely, the less regenerated men will be through faith, the less the social life of the church will conform to the plan of God and the less satisfactory will be the political order (expressed through law and customs).

We can see that the faithful presence of the church is indispensable to social life and all its aspects. The church ought to be a leaven inspiring and generating social, political, and economic life. If the church is dead, if the church exists but is not the community of the members of the body of Christ, if the church is present but does not impart to society as a whole the impulse of her constant regeneration by God's Word, the church herself co-operates in the propagation of social disorder.

Yet on its side the state (which by laws and by constraint ought to enforce the political order) has no guarantee against its own decay and corruption. If a real church is not there constantly to remind the state of its mission, the very state becomes a factor of disorder. As a matter of fact, by itself the state does not know God's order. It belongs to the church to witness God's order to governments.

The problem of whether or not state officials ought to be personally Christian after all is not very important. Of course, Calvin wished that magistrates be Christian. But in encouraging persecuted churches, Calvin has shown that the Christian's obedience to state officials in no way depends on the faith or un-faith of these authorities. For, whatever be the political or religious opinions professed by governments, Christians must respect the historical political order in which they have to live. This order is indispensable to the social life to which they belong. Moreover, through their political activity, Christians ought to participate actively in the continuous restoration of the political order. The reason is that no order (whatever it be) ever attains the perfection which God desires for humanity.

But is the submission which Christians owe to the state unconditional and unlimited? Certainly not.

Calvin is one of the Christian thinkers who has best established the right and duty of resisting the state. Under whatever political regime Christians be, they ought to oppose with vigor state demands each time these demands are contrary to the will of God. According to Calvin, this right to resist the state cannot be legally taken away. This typically Calvinian right to resistance is not in contradiction to the imperative Christian duty to submit to authorities. On the contrary, it expresses the necessary limits of this duty. The reason is that, at all times and in all circumstances, the Christian has only one Lord and Master, and he is Jesus Christ. The partial obedience which the Christian owes to his human masters, to his parents, to his teachers, to his wife or husband, to his employers, to his military superiors, and to state officials is only a derived and conditional obedience which is at all times subordinated to the only absolute authority: that of Jesus Christ.

The Christian's political resistance could never involve a global or total opposition to a government. Prophetic witnessing is always to definite and precise points. If this resistance brings persecution upon itself, the Christian church ought to gather her courage and never despair. The church knows indeed that by remaining faithful in all things, she is the first to contribute to safeguarding society with which she is solidary, that is, one solid. In this way, and in the deepest and noblest sense of the word, the church performs a civic and patriotic work.

At each moment and in each situation, therefore, the real church and the vigilant Christians aware of their obedience to Christ ought always and ever anew to discern between the points on which they ought to base and fortify the regime in power and the points which they ought to resist.

A consequence of the political teaching of Calvin is that a Christian, except in altogether exceptional cases, cannot be a radical revolutionary seeking to uproot the social order in which he lives. On the other hand, the Christian cannot be completely conservative. The reason is that, by definition and nature, the Christian is a continual re-former of both state and church. These are ever to be re-formed according to the spirit found in the gospel. In other words, the Christian always and evermore seeks to conform the life of his city and religious community to the orders of God.

In summary, when Christians are aware of the responsibility flowing from their faith, they are under obligation to participate actively in political life.

Basically they are to do so in the following three ways:

First, by contributing through personal engagement to set up a Christian community within the city and seeing to it that this religious community be, as far as possible, faithful to the gospel. This is by far the most important contribution to the civic life of the land and proof of the most enlightened patriotism.

Secondly, by personally engaging oneself in political action with a view of bettering social life through legal and institutional means.

Finally, by energetically refusing to follow the state each time that it imposes duties which are incompatible with the demands of the gospel.

At this juncture we must point out that in the name of the Christian faith, Calvin energetically opposed the state's using arms, even in those circumstances when military interventions seemed humanly justified.

For example, Calvin firmly rejected all recourses to war against the government of states although they were considered enemies of the faith and did cruelly persecute Protestants within their borders.

Like the Reformer Zwingli, Calvin denounced the misdeeds of mercenary military service even though it brought wealth and glory to the Swiss.

Calvin justified recourse to arms only when such action was necessary for the defense of a legitimate state. In our last chapter we shall return to this question.

This scheme of relations between state and church is a marked characteristic of Calvinian teaching, and it has been very often disfigured. It is absolutely wrong to say, for example, that Calvin established a theocracy in Geneva. The reason is that the idea of an identity of state and church never entered the mind of Calvin. And we must remember that Calvin never exercised any political office. On the contrary, all his life he struggled against the encroachments of the state which wished to bring the church under subjection.

On the other hand, we can rightly censure Calvin with having solicited the intervention of secular power in sanctioning disciplinary measures of the church. The drama of Michel Servetus illustrates Calvin's error. Yet this excess can be explained by the exceptionally and now easily overlooked hard times in which our Reformer lived. Moreover, and in all truth, this error can be corrected on the basis of the very teaching of Calvin. This shows that his error is accidental rather than fundamental. In our last chapter we shall consider which of Calvin's teachings are, in our opinion, still valid today, and which may be left aside.

II

MONEY AND PROPERTY

It has been said that the thought and work of Calvin have inspired his followers with the most uncompromising social conservatism as well as with the boldest revolutionary socialism. As a matter of fact, it is established that political and social movements of very diverse orientations, sometimes even violently opposed one to the other, have appealed to Calvin in order to justify themselves. The reality is that each of these movements has taken inspiration, in perfectly good faith, from that portion of Calvin's writings which justified its program and has left aside (of the immense and subtle work of the Reformer) that which was contrary to its platform. Thus a certain Calvinistic tradition, orthodox on the theological plane and conservative on the political plane, has stamped certain Protestant societies with the dreadful character of spiritual and social immobility, thereby covering up and often masking an aggressive and unrestrained economic activity. Yet it is equally true that several wholesome movements of social Christianity have received their impetus from Calvin's dynamic interpretation of the spiritual liberty of the gospel. These movements of course were concerned not with abstract theology, but with social progress.

If we consider closely not only the thought but also the personal activity of Calvin as well, and if we look not at a mere portion of his thought and action but rather at their totality, we shall realize that the work of this master may be defined as a social personalism.

The reason, based on the gospel, is that Calvin's preoccupation was to assure for man a total unfolding of personal life. The Reformer wanted to guarantee fully the brotherhood and solidarity which unite men one to the other in Christ.

In our first chapter we have sketched the premises of this social personalism. We must now examine the place and role which Calvin gives to money, and the significance which he assigns to property.

1. Economic and Social Life at the Time of Calvin

In the sixteenth century, Western society was in full effervescence. We leave aside the religious struggles since they are already known to our readers. These religious struggles were not the only factor in rupturing the old world. Society was exploding under the thrust of innumerable sociological forces. First of all, bloody military struggles of many monarchs who were jealous of their individual prestige had broken society to pieces. Europe had almost continuously been ravaged by the Hundred Years War, by the Burgundian Wars, and by the wars in Italy. Society moreover was bursting under the thrust of social revolutionary movements unclenched by an upsetting economic transformation.

The discoveries of the New World had, in effect, given to Europe floods of gold which fecundated innumerable industries and multiplied commercial exchanges.

The ancient corporation structures and frames could no longer either contain or orient this superabundant activity. An uncontrolled capitalism was born and rapidly developed outside the ancient urban centers of production. This capitalistic development brought about a vertiginous increase in cost of living as well as a cheapening of labor. It caused a rapid proletarization (that is, a mass of indigent wage-earners) in both city and country. Large fortunes piled up and multiplied while the miserable masses became ever more prolific.

The invention of the printing press, then the pre-Reformation, and finally the Reformation gave the leaven of the gospel (that is, its spreading and transforming influence) back to the people. But this leaven no longer acted upon these tormented masses as a pious consolation justifying the injustices of the great and the oppression by the mighty, but rather as an energetic stimulant which gave to believers the courage to think and to speak the truth. We admit, of course, that these manifestations were often incoherent, as the Anabaptists' extravagances show.

Everything concurred to precipitate both in the church and in society a profound inner seething out of which, through much suffering and bloodshed, were to issue radical transformations and irreversible social changes.

The convergent action of these external subversions (which were breaking down the old medieval structures of society) and of the inner renewal of faith (which was in contact with the newly rediscovered gospel) were to lead the church as a whole toward an entirely new understanding of social problems.

An opening up of personal religion toward the world and a parallel invasion of theological thought by social problems formed a definite characteristic and turning point of the Reformation at this time.

Although he had no monopoly in this matter, Calvin gave an entirely new expression to this change of religious orientation. At the time of the Reformation an intense development of secular orders shows that there existed in the Roman Church the same need of integrating world problems with the life of faith.

This was a new phenomenon in comparison with medieval personal religion, which ran away from the world. The sudden advent and prodigious expansion of the Jesuits, for example, is a striking and typical illustration of what we are saying.

Yet nothing better illustrates this transformation and opening of the Christian faith, thought, and action to social problems than the conversion of Calvin himself when he decided to leave the Roman Church and to enter the new faith.

Until 1533 (the probable year of this change), Calvin leads the studious and conventional life of a Catholic bourgeois. Being open to new ideas and an authentic intellectual, like the human-ist reformers of Roman milieu, Calvin's well-balanced faith dreads the subversion of conventions and scorns the revolutionary mood of the earliest small Evangelical groups. For Calvin, re-ligious faith, on the one hand, and society, on the other, are two

separate domains which have no correspondence and no correla-
tion except on the plane of his individual ethics. If we want to be
sure that this really was once the outlook of Calvin, all we have to
do is to read the work which he published at this time—his
exposition of the *De Clementia* of Seneca.

But once converted, Calvin suddenly and with impetuous
liberty intervenes in favor of those men whom the king and
ruling classes held to be dangerous revolutionaries and subver-
sives. His letter to François I, which is found at the head of the
first edition of the *Christian Institutes,* written in the spring of
1535, opened the public career of our Reformer. In it, Calvin very
vigorously attacks those men who refuse to see that the gospel
requires in this life a great deal from men and demands great
sacrifices in political and secular matters. Calvin does not separate
faith and world as two domains—one as religious and the other
as profane. For the re-formed Christian, concern for the secular
city is a direct expression of his Christian faithfulness. We shall
become more aware of this as we now proceed to study in brief
Calvin's thought concerning money, wealth, and property.

2. *Money as Instrument of God.*

According to re-formed Christian thought, economic goods
and material wealth are values directly bound to the Christian
faith and closely associated with spiritual life.

As a Christian who strictly bases himself on the gospel, Calvin
knows nothing about that pagan antagonism which opposes pre-
tended spiritual values to material realities. Calvin repudiates
that age-long struggle which, since ancient times, contrasts spir-
itualism and materialism. Under the impulsion of Western and
Communist ideologies, this struggle and contrast have today
become again acute.

Referring himself to Scripture, our Reformer teaches that
material goods are instruments of God's providence. As money
represents these goods, money is the means which God uses in
granting to man what is necessary to the support of the existence
of man and his companions. God puts wealth at the disposal of

man so that he may organize his life and the life of society for which he is solidarily responsible as well.

Further, by dispensing all material goods and particularly money to his creature, the Creator makes himself known as a life-giving Father. Money therefore does not have a merely utilitarian function. It has really a spiritual mission. It is a sign of the grace of God who makes his children live. Moreover, money is a sign of the Kingdom of God. Just as the wealth of the Promised Land was, for Israel, a prefiguration of the opulence of the future life, so money is a sign of the abundance in the world to come. As such, money is a sign with a twofold meaning: It is a sign of grace for him who through faith acknowledges that all his possessions come to him from God, but it is also a sign of condemnation of him who gets the goods of his living without discerning that they are a gift of God.

Hence money always puts man to a test. By want, God tests some men to find out whether or not in poverty they truly put their trust in him. Do men, who are of course faithfully working for their living, expect only from God's faithful providence what is necessary for the support of their lives? Or do men, in the last resort, believe that it is their working strength alone which can make them live?

Yet by abundance, by prosperity, or by simple comfort, God equally puts to proof other men in order to measure their faith. Being rich or merely at ease, do they still place their whole trust in God? Or rather, has money deceived them to the point of having them believe that money has really a power independent of God?

God reads the answer to this question in the use which man makes of his riches. For it is the employment of our money which exactly and mathematically translates to the eyes of God our real faith, and it does this far better than our fine words and pious feelings.

In the scale of values according to God, there is therefore no kind of correspondence between the spiritual and moral worth of a man, and his wealth or poverty. The judgment of God is not according to the current standards of our bourgeois ethics.

What we have just said might let us believe that the gospel purely and simply justifies the individual appropriation of money and economic goods—some men getting more and others getting less according to the sole arbitrary dispensation of the providence of God.

Things really do not go this way.

We have previously indicated that, in the purpose of God, man is not an individual, but rather a person whose harmonious development is closely related to the development of society. Man is a social being and wholly solidary with other men.

We have also indicated that this solidarity is particularly and concretely expressed in a mutual exchange of goods and services.

According to the purpose of God, the unequal distribution of wealth among men is not arbitrarily destined to favor some men at the expense of others. On the contrary, the function of this inequality is to provoke a continuous redistribution of goods. This redistribution goes from the richer toward the poorer.

Life according to God, the social life, is an uninterrupted circulation of goods, concretely expressing men's complementary life and obligatory solidarity.

This circulation is naturally assured by economic exchanges which are made necessary by the division of labor. Later we shall speak of division of work as further expression of human solidarity.

According to the purpose of God, there is another motive in the circulation of wealth. It is love. And love causes the unselfish gift which goes from the rich toward the poor. According to the vision of life found in the Gospels, the rich is he who, with regard to his neighbor, finds himself in a privileged position whatever the amount of his wealth may be. A man is always rich to somebody.

The rich man has a providential economic mission. He is charged with sharing a part of his wealth with a man poorer than himself so that the poor will no longer be poor and the rich will no longer be rich. On the other hand, the poor man also has a spiritual mission to fulfill. The poor is destined to be the neighbor of the rich, to be the one who, on the part of God, offers the rich an opportunity of ridding himself of his goods and freeing himself from monetary slavery.

In a society ordered according to the purpose of God, there is, therefore, a mutual communication of goods. This communication does not completely eliminate, but rather it attenuates, economic inequalities. If nothing fettered and clogged this free circulation of wealth, society would, through a continuous movement of reciprocity flowing from human solidarity, tend toward a relative economic equality. This equality would be differentiated according to the real vocation of each person. When we shall later speak of work and legitimate hierarchies, we will see that all men indeed do not have the same vocation.

Calvin has strongly insisted on this mutual communication of wealth within society. As a model, he took the redistribution of the manna among the Israelites. This redistribution tended toward a differentiated equality according to which (to use again an expression of the apostle Paul) "he who has gathered much had not too much, and he who has gathered little had not too little" (II Cor. 8:15). Hence Calvin calls the rich "the ministers of the poor." The poor are sent on the part of God to the rich in order to test the faith and charity of the rich. Calvin calls the poor the "receivers of God," the "vicars of Christ," the "proxies" or "solicitors of God."

Consequently Calvin notes that, according to the Gospels, theft is not only the act of grabbing something belonging to another person. Theft is first of all refusing to give to our neighbor that which love ought to give to him. Theft is keeping for oneself that which rightly ought to be returned to others on the part of God and according to the order of charity.

Unfortunately this order of love, this order of God, has suffered grave perturbations in the world. Evil ravages society to the point that the right order of economic goods is destroyed. Money escapes the function which God had assigned to it. That which was the instrument of God (and is called to become again the instrument of God) was transformed into an instrument of Mammon's domination.

3. Money as Instrument of Social Oppression and Economic Disorder

We have previously seen that seeking an illusory freedom away from God brought man into subjection to sin and vitiation of his humanness. Calvin has shown that this depravity (that is, this crookedness of the person) entailed the perversion of the whole society.

Man's responsibility as manager before and for God permitted man to make a good use of material goods, wealth, and money.

This responsibility, however, was annihilated by the action of the evil one and by the effect of sin. Henceforth money took the place of God in the heart of sinful man, of the natural man who we all are when we are not renewed by Christ. Money becomes the instrument of evil. A combination of money and evil now rules over creation.

The Bible calls the power of money thus made god "Mammon."

As always, Satan is very clever. The making a god of money seldom shows up as a coarse idolatry. The men who consciously worship money are rare. Satan insinuates himself into man's heart in a far more subtle way. All Satan does is to suggest to man that, after all, it is money and not God which assures the daily bread and guarantees man's future. Thus Mammon secretly takes the place of God. Once this place is occupied, in order the better to deceive man, Mammon allows man full liberty to practice his own religion and to say his prayers. He even suggests to man to make two parts of his life: that of spiritual things to which goes all the devotion of man, and that of material things which absorbs all the preoccupations of man. The most important thing is not to mix the two domains! Beware of associating faith and business, money and religion! This dualism is typically pagan and is profoundly anchored in the heart of man. When this dualism emerges in the church, it is a sure sign that, as a matter of fact, the church is in subjection to Mammon. We cannot have two goals, that is, as Jesus says, a man cannot in practice serve two such incompatible masters as God and money. "Gold and silver are mine," says the eternal Lord. And if gold and silver do not belong to the Lord, if they do not overtly enter into the life of faith and into worship, it means that they belong to Mammon.

Now, the victory of Mammon over man does not produce only the crookedness of the individual; it immediately also brings about the perversion of society and church. Immense perturbations follow in economic life, engendering social disorder. Selfish appropriation of wealth, hoarding, cornering, monopolization, greed, and avarice as well as waste, prodigality, luxury, or absence of sobriety—visible expressions of sin—block the harmonious circulation of goods foreseen in God's order. These disorders falsify the just repartition and distribution of money within creation according to the purpose of God. They clog an equitable redistribution of the benefits of wealth among all. Misery and luxury together, and between them the social irresponsibility of the moderate individualist, are the sign of this fundamental vitiation of society.

Yet as we have said before, neither world nor society is mercilessly abandoned to disorder. God intervenes in economic history in order to re-establish just human relations. And right human relations flow from man's right relations with God. On the cross of Golgotha until the triumph of his Resurrection, Jesus wages a victorious combat against evil. From rich Lord which he was, the man Jesus made himself poor, yet retaining the power over all the visible and invisible riches of the world. And to humanity Calvin offers this man Jesus as the exemplar of social man.

Jesus' voluntary poverty, his free dispensing to all humanity the goods of creation of which he is the sovereign Lord, opens for the world the way to its social and economic restoration.

4. The Function of Money Re-established in the Church

In the real church when she is truly the community of the members of the body of Christ, we find the priming of the world's social restoration.

Associated with Christ through faith and restored into his dignity as a child of God, man finds again a right relation to his neighbor. That man receives a new and exact understanding of the role of money. Money is an instrument of God for the support and subsistence of society. That man understands also that money must be mastered in order to be consecrated to God and to one's neighbor. On the personal plane, this rediscovery imposes first a rigorous discipline on man.

With regard to the new life of the Christian, we have spoken of a certain asceticism. This asceticism is particularly exercised in the use of money.

Concerning this, let us note that Calvin has peculiarly transformed Christian asceticism. In the Middle Ages, asceticism had a meritorious value. Through asceticism, man acquired merits which were indispensable for his salvation.

But the Reformers gave an altogether different value to asceticism. They had discovered in the Gospels the good message of free forgiveness—of deliverance through grace. Christ's sacrifice is the only merit of which we can avail ourselves before God.

Nevertheless, dying unto oneself and the new life which communion with Christ brings about impose upon man a discipline which involves his whole life. This asceticism is a consequence of salvation and no longer its precondition. Asceticism is the result of sanctification "without which no one shall see the Lord."

There has been in history a style of material life which imposed itself on Christians each time that they took the Word of God seriously. Such a style had characterized the primitive church; and it marked also the Reformed churches since their beginning.

It is also with his money that the Christian renders to God a worship in spirit and in truth. For the Christian, the act of offering is an essential spiritual act, a priming, an act of worship in the highest degree. Indeed by his offering the believer certifies to God that Mammon has been dethroned. By concrete gifts, the Christian expresses to God the real measure of his faith. By these gifts, the man confesses that his Lord is really the acknowledged Master of his entire life—moral, physical, and material. And the

church which has understood this cannot be contented in worship with a collection which is not an act of offering, but is, in
one way or another, dissimulated behind the singing of a hymn
or at the exit of the faithful. The Christian community must
certify by an explicit public act that for the church, money has
been exorcised by the eternal Christ, that money has been stripped
of its evil spiritual power and has recovered its true function
as servant.

The rediscovery of this function of money has immediate
social repercussions. In the church, the new spiritual communion
which Christ establishes between the members of his body leads
them necessarily to a mutual communication of their goods. This
redistribution is done according to the possibilities and according
to the needs of each person. As Calvin says, "God wills that there
be proportion and equality among us, that is, each man is to
provide for the needy according to the extent of his means, so that
no man has too much and no man has too little."

In the new society which Christ's church forms, individual
property is not abolished. This property, however, is put at the
disposal and at the service of all. When some members of the
Christian community are in contact with the living Christ and
truly live by the communion with the eternal Christ, there
results such a reciprocity that a new medium level is established
among all the members of that community. The crying differences
between rich and poor thus disappear. A spontaneous redistribution of goods is a direct consequence of communion with Christ.
In a way which approaches the ideal social order we have de-
scribed, this redistribution re-establishes that equilibrium or balance of wealth of which we have spoken. God truly wills the
re-establishment of that equilibrium or balance of riches which sin
has destroyed.

"This communication which Christ has established among the
members of his body," Calvin writes, "ought to encourage us to
be more prompt, more active, and more diligent in doing good to
others. For there ought to be an order or system of proportional
right in the church, as I have indicated above. And it is this—
that when the members spiritually communicate, one to another,

according to the measure of whatever gifts they have from God and the necessity of others, this mutual conferring of goods ought to produce a strong and befitting proportion. This produces even a fine harmony, though some possess more and others less, and gifts are distributed unequally . . . Thus communication in the church consists in this—that each person acquits himself of whatever in charity he owes to his neighbors."

In order to realize this particular church ministry of mutual communication of goods among all, Calvin creates anew the service of the diaconate. In imitation of the primitive church, Calvin had money re-enter the circuit of spiritual life. Calvin gave back to economic goods the reason for their existence, and he gave to economics a ministry on earth. The deacons were charged with the duty of re-establishing among the members of the community that circulation of economic goods which ought to show the spiritual solidarity of the members of the body of Christ. All are responsible—one to another—for the spiritual life, the material condition, and the physical health of others. And they turn even to the exterior to bring to the Protestant poor abroad the service and testimony owed to the needy according to God's will.

We recall that as soon as the Reformation came, it brought in Geneva the institution of a general hospital as well as assistance to the sick, the aged, and the invalid. Calvin perfected this system. He insisted that this assistance (organized and managed by the state but exercised by the ecclesiastical ministry of the deacons) knew no national discrimination. He extended this assistance to people at home and included a social medical service. "Let there be a physician and a surgeon hired by the city," say the Ordinances of 1541, "who be held to take care of the hospital and visit the other poor."

Calvin's preaching about money is extremely bold and to the point. It encourages the poor and stimulates the liberality of believers. It proves to be vehement against the rich who greedily keep their riches and against the speculators who, to enrich themselves, keep away from the market (until prices go up) those goods which society needs. Calvin's sermons are set against the insolent luxury of some men who, without regard for the poverty of others, waste the common patrimony which God has given for the good of all.

The preaching of Calvin, however, is only an aspect of his activity. The modesty in which he and his ministerial colleagues live is proverbial. It nears poverty. And Calvin's proceedings in favor of the disinherited are unceasing. He harasses the state councils so that they make provisions to relieve the needy. After the massacre of the Protestants of Provence in 1545, for instance, Calvin himself organized a general collection. He climbs the winding stairways of buildings crowded with refugees in order to collect the contribution of each.

If, in the church of believers restored by the life in Christ and faith, money recovers its just function of service, it must find again a similar place in society as a whole. Calvin thinks that it belongs to the state to bring this about.

5. Property Safeguarded and Limited by the State

According to Calvin's teachings, the state has the mission to make an order (nearing as much as possible the divine order) reign among sinful men.

While the living Christ re-establishes this order of God among the members of his church who let the divine Word guide them, the state must tend partially to restore that order in society as a whole.

For Calvin, the political mission of the state implies a certain intervention in economics.

The state is to do this not by force, not as the producer, but as the regulator of economic exchanges and distribution of the benefits of wealth. If the state were not this regulator, sin would destroy the good functioning of economic life. Hoarding and monopolies obstruct the circulation of goods among men, while waste deprives society of wealth.

The sumptuary laws of Geneva are famous. They limited luxury and private expenditures in the interest of the state. Most of these laws were not made by Calvin but by his successors. The sumptuary laws were inspired as much by economic politics as by social ethics.

Calvin's thought was that society ought to keep the use of material goods within just limits and to orient the destination of material goods toward social mutual aid. The sumptuary laws translated this will of Calvin. We must not forget that at the time of Calvin Geneva was encircled on all sides by Catholic peoples. The problems of the daily bread and of the material survival of the population of Geneva were then terribly acute. If we are to understand the sumptuary laws, we must not judge them according to the standards of bourgeois morality and of worldly life. We must consider these laws in their historical setting. Then we can see that they were dictated by a rigorous war economy.

With reference to riches or wealth, the function of the state may normally be briefly defined as follows: If order must reign, the state must guarantee private property. But the state must keep watch that this property be not acquired at the expense of the property of other men, and that it be put at the service of the collectivity. For Calvin, ownership of a good is not absolute. It is limited and conditional. For a standard, Calvin does not hesitate to quote the ancient Jewish law which foresaw a periodical redistribution of lands and liberation from debts to the end that property should never (through individual hoarding and general involvement in debt) become a source of social oppression.

6. Criticism of Calvin's Thought

This short sketch of our Reformer's doctrine about money, economics, and society shows that, in many respects, Calvin's thought in these matters is close to the minds both of his predecessors and of medieval theologians. Even as they do, so does he denounce the spiritual danger which riches constitute. Calvin also, as they, justifies the possession of a material good insofar as it not only supports its owner and his family but serves the needs of society as a whole. For Calvin and his predecessors, moderation, the duty of mutual aid, and in former days the obligation to give alms were preconditions to legitimate property.

Yet Calvin clearly differs from medieval theology in matters of voluntary poverty. Considered in itself, asceticism brings no extra merit to him who practices it. The life of faith does not imply a medieval turning away from material goods. On the contrary, spiritual life implies that the believer is to assume, before God, full and entire responsibility for the material life, not only of himself, but also of the whole of society as well. Far from being ejected from the horizon of faith, money is made a servant of spiritual life. Money is consciously and fully domesticated. This subjection of money to faith leads to that evangelical simplicity and even to that austerity which have characterized the style of Calvinian life. In no way does Calvin deny the spiritual value of privation and sacrifice. But, as we have said before, in no case are these for him meritorious deeds.

This theological rehabilitation of material life breaks away from the ancient Christian tradition of contrasting spirit and matter. Though Christianity has never succeeded in completely ridding itself of the traditional spirit-matter contrast, Calvin's Christian rehabilitation of our physical life will have considerable repercussions in the economic life of Protestant societies.

If we consider Calvin's doctrine of wealth in the light of modern science, we ought to marvel at seeing how prophetic his discernment was. It took several centuries for the science of economics to find anew the decisive role of the circulation of goods in maintaining social order, which Calvin had so clearly seen.

One may, however, reproach Calvin with not having given sufficient importance to saving as a new source of productivity. Haunted by the dread of miserliness, avarice, and hoarding, Calvin had not clearly seen the economic value of capitalization, although he justified its principle when discussing loans at interest. We shall consider this point in our next chapter.

One may also note Calvin's clairvoyance in discerning that social order can be had only in a constant equilibrium between personal economic responsibility and state control. After the passionate ideological struggle between socialism and bourgeoisism, the present world at large walks in fact toward an empirical social personalism which is something quite close to the equilibrium sponsored by Calvin.

The restoration of the function of money in the church, however, proves to be the most evangelical and realistic of Calvin's teachings for our day. Our evangelical churches had entirely forgotten this aspect of Calvin's social and ecclesiastical teaching.

III

WORK, SALARY, COMMERCE, AND BANKING

Almost all of the various economic goods which God uses for the subsistence of the society of men are also the product of the work of men.

1. The Work of Man as a Work of God

The work of man, the strength of work which a man can develop, is the very work through which God provides for the life of his creatures. It is the work of God. For a man, to act correctly is in all things to align himself with the action of God. The work of man has a meaning because, when rightly accomplished, it is the very work of God by which God supports the life of his creatures.

Now, like all things, this human work is vitiated by sin. It participates in the great disorder of creation. By freeing himself from his voluntary obedience to God, man disposes of his work in an autonomous way. Detached from the work of God, man's work immediately becomes a source of pain, of worry, of injustice, and of oppression.

If work is to become again true work, if work is to find again its original meaning, if work is to be no longer a source of oppression but a service, if work is to give satisfaction to the worker, man must personally associate himself anew with the work of God; he must align himself with the divine activity which Providence in the world pursues in order to nourish man.

To reach that condition, man must keep silence, stop his own activity, let himself be possessed by God, and turn over to God the management of his work.

Such is the meaning and bearing of rest, of Sabbath, and of sanctification.

The repose or rest of man has no value in itself. The only reason that rest is prescribed to man is to put him in condition in order that he may have access to the labor of God. "Because the Lord," says Calvin, "has not simply commanded men to rest every seventh day as if he took pleasure in their idleness. What pleases God is the fact that being freed from all other business, we more freely apply our minds to recognize and acknowledge the Creator of the world."

"The faithful must rest from their works in order to let God do his work in them."

This putting man again at his place before God is possible only through the mediation of the eternal and living Christ.

To find again the right meaning of his work, man must enter the communion with God which only Christ gives. Man therefore must pass through repentance and personally engage himself in the communion of the church. Man is thus sanctified—restored opposite God.

For the people of Israel, this sanctification took place on the Sabbath day. But since Christ has come, and since every day he acts in the entire world through his Holy Spirit, man is sanctified by his daily communion with the Resurrected One. Man's sanctification takes place every day. Thus the Sabbath is abolished because the Sabbath is no longer necessary.

Yet in order that the common sanctification of the Christian community be exercised, a particular day must be set so that the assembly may meet. To that end the early Christians selected Sunday—the memorial day of the Resurrection.

Personal and communal sanctification re-establishes man in the order and action of God. Man's work becomes again a part of the work of God. And at the same time, man finds again the right social relations with his neighbor.

This is the reason why the command to sanctify the day of rest mentions labor relations—the intercourse between masters and servants.

Thus restored and reintegrated in the great work of God,

work becomes again creative and liberating. Work ceases to be an occasion of oppression and division. Man's sanctification by the living Christ confers the most eminent dignity upon work.

Contrariwise, the profanation of Sunday practically means the scorning of the sanctification offered by Christ and is at the origin of the corruption of work.

By associating man with his own labor, God assigns an earthly goal to his creature. Man is created to work. Here on earth, man accomplishes his destiny in working.

Consequently, idleness is against nature. Idleness is a form of human alienation. For man, it means refusal of his divine vocation, his rupture with God. Idleness is therefore an offense to God. "The blessing of the Lord," says Calvin, "is on the hands of him who works. Certainly God curses laziness and loafing." Hence Calvin denounces the fault of those men who draw their resources from the work of others without bringing a real service to the community. He decries those "idlers and good-for-nothing individuals who live by the sweat of others and yet bring no common means to help mankind."

Since work is this indispensable operation by which man becomes accomplished in his obedience to God and without which man is neither a man nor a Christian, unemployment is a social scourge which must be fought and denounced with extreme vigor. For to deprive man of his work is truly a crime. As a matter of fact, it is equivalent to taking away his life.

"Though we receive our food from the hand of God," Calvin writes, "he has ordained that we work. Is now work taken away? Behold, the life of man is thrown under!"

"Concerning artisans and workingmen, we know that all their income comes from their being able to earn their living . . . Now, it is as if God has put their life in their hands, that is to say, in their work. To deprive them of this necessary means is equivalent to cutting their throats."

For Calvin, moreover, to abuse the work of others or to exploit them is a crime. "For, there are men who would be happy to kill in three days a poor person in their service. It is all the same to them, provided they get a profit. Now, on the contrary, God declares unto us that we must treat those who labor for us with such humanity that they be not burdened beyond measure in order that they may continue to labor and have occasion to thank God for their work."

God wishes "to correct the cruelty of the rich who employ poor people in their service and yet do not sufficiently compensate them for their labor."

Calvin found in Geneva a propitious place in which to apply his doctrine. Before Calvin, measures had already been taken to regulate the length of work time. Sunday had been declared a public holiday, while the other ancient celebrations and holidays (on which people did not work) had been suppressed. Vagrancy had been forbidden. Every man had been ordered to have a trade and to make a living.

But the arrival of innumerable Protestant refugees in Geneva created delicate and complex work problems for the city. Calvin faced these difficulties with exemplary clearness of thought. He was concerned about the professional education of youth as well as about the readjustment of adults to new employments. The men who could not immediately find a place in their professions were assigned to remunerative temporary jobs. But not all refugees could be reintegrated in the existing professions. Hence new trades were created. Calvin intervenes at the so-called Small Council so that it may develop the weaving industry. A silk-winder from Lyons becomes the instructor of young people who had remained dependent on the General Hospital. In addition to the sick, the hospital must also accept the resourceless poor. Then a man from Lucca establishes the manufacturing of silk-tissues. Later, other refugees, not satisfied with just this aspect of the industry, want to produce the silk itself. Hence they will introduce the culture of mulberry trees and the raising of silk-worms (which feed only on mulberry leaves). Calvin intervenes for the solution of other labor problems connected with remuner-ation, problems which we will consider in our section on salary.

As for a doctrine of work, we must note that Calvin was an innovator with reference to his predecessors. These conformed to Christian medieval doctrines and considered work an earthly duty having no immediate connection with faith and spiritual life. The duty to work was inspired by a natural ethics and a natural order. By its giving priority to contemplation over action, Scholasticism moreover had contributed to strip professional activities of all prestige and all spiritual value. Calvin, on the contrary, strictly ties work to the Christian life. He emphasizes that the gospel makes labor a participation in the work of God. Calvin thus confers to human work a spiritual dignity and value which it never had before. This fact will have considerable economic repercussions in the rise and development of Calvinist societies.

2. *Salary as a Gift of God*

To understand the spiritual significance of salary, we must recall a fundamental truth of the gospel: Man has no right to remuneration from God. Anything that man receives is due to the grace of the Savior God who by pure loving-kindness provides for the support of man. "Properly speaking," Calvin says, "God does not owe anything to any person."

"Whatever duty we may fulfill, God is under no obligation to pay us a salary."

Yet, in his goodness, God does not abandon us without giving us what we need. He remunerates our work, not out of obligation, but rather out of love. "Out of his free goodness God offers us a salary . . . He rewards our labor which yet is due to him without remuneration."

Whatever be the method of remuneration, the human salary granted to our work is therefore the tangible expression of the gratuitous and unmerited salary with which God honors our labor.

Hence the salary has something sacred. It expresses in a visible way God's intervention in favor of our existence. Salary is the concrete sign of God's providence which meets our vital needs. It certifies that God is at work, saving and feeding his children.

Since this salary is the sign of the grace of God, man cannot dispose of it according to his fancy. The salary of his neighbor does not belong to him. In giving to his dependent workingman his dues, the employer simply remits to his neighbor that which God himself bestows upon the man so that he may live. To confiscate or to hold the whole or part of a salary coming to others is a sacrilege. It is an offense to God as well as to our neighbor.

Moreover, speaking objectively, the salary belongs neither to the employer nor to the workingman. Both receive it from God and both ought to receive it as coming from God. Such is the preliminary condition for determining a just salary. Its exact amount can be established only if the partners (employer and employee) are aware that they are fully responsible before God for the fruits which they receive from their goods and from their work. In this case they must set the amount of the salary by common agreement, freely, with full awareness of their responsibility.

This prick of spiritual conscience with regard to salary can only come to birth in faith. Now, since not all men have faith, a human correspondence to this gauge of a just salary must be found.

The right price is either the market price or the price fixed by authorities. But every Christian must know that this human norm is quite relative. Considering the social disorder in which the world lives, the human standard cannot be absolutely trusted. At any given moment, customs and laws always reflect, more or less, this disorder. The objective setting of a price in one way or the other does not release the Christian from his responsibility toward the man who, above or below him, works with or for him.

When the labor market is saturated, it is especially illicit to let the salary level drop down below the amount which a man and his family normally need for a living. "For behold what the rich often do," says Calvin; "they spy for occasions and opportunities to cut down by half the wages of poor people who need employment. 'This man is completely destitute,' the rich murmurs at seeing a poor unemployed; 'I will have him for a morsel of bread because, in spite of his opposition, he shall have to put himself at my mercy. I will give him half-wages, and he shall have to be contented with it.' When we use such hardness, even though we do not retain his salary, we are truly cruel and we defraud a poor man."

To avoid the frequent quarrels about remuneration, Calvin suggests the salary contract. He even thinks of collective contracts and recommends arbitration before the courts.

Though Calvin holds the revolt of exploited men and their recourse to violence illegitimate, our Reformer confirms that God often uses the disobedience of workingmen as a means of judging and of chastising exploiters. Calvin is not opposed to non-violent protests and strikes. For, "what greater violence can we find," Calvin writes, "than that which by hunger and poverty starves those who feed us by their labor? And yet such a strange cruelty is quite common. For, many men have a tyrannical nature and think that mankind has been made only for them. Now, Saint James says that the salary of the laborer cries because anything that men withhold wrongfully or by fraud, or by violence or force, loudly demands vengeance. We must note that Saint James adds that the cry of the poor reaches up to the ears of God so that we may know that the wrongs done to the poor will not remain unpunished."

In this quest for a just remuneration, the Reformer Calvin, as well as his colleagues in Geneva, has shown an astonishing social activity. Calvin may be seen several times going to authorities in order to obtain from them salary raises for workingmen and teachers. When the City Council votes family allowances to ministers, Calvin demands that the state support the orphans. And in order that the labor of minors be not misused, the council decrees that a patrol will, in the name of the sovereign state of Geneva, see to it that the balance of salaries due to children shall be duly paid to them.

Calvin's times were difficult. They were marked by a general and vertiginous rise in the cost of living. This rise was not compensated by a corresponding rise in salaries. This situation caused, in certain trades as well as in the countryside, the birth of a sort of proletariat which became turbulent at times. To protect themselves against these hard times, artisans and workers organized

secret brotherhoods of companions which authorities in vain
tried to dissolve. In certain places, strikes (in which Protestants
were particularly active) broke out. Such were the strikes of
printers at Lyons in 1539. They were due to insufficient salaries as
well as to a bad distribution of working hours. Thanks to the
organization of labor forces and their control over trades, the
movement of protest expanded and reached Paris. The employers
had recourse to authorities, but the workers persevered and
finally gained their cause. To avoid social troubles, the edict of
Villers-Cotterêts (1539) prohibits unions; but the French authorities do not succeed in dissolving the workers' secret organizations
which were formed by laborers condemned to misery. Their poverty was made worse by the fact that the authorities, wishing to
stop prices from going up, imposed ceiling salaries.

In Geneva, where the organization of corporations was much
later than elsewhere, the state intervenes with the same measures.
In 1559 the council sets a maximum salary for workingmen and
then takes away their right to organize unions. This repression
of liberty causes the unanimous discontent of workers and un-
clenches social troubles. What are the spiritual directors of the
city doing then? They intervene in the debate among workers,
employers, and authorities, and suggest an equalitarian organization of trades. In 1559, on the initiative of the ministers, the
council, in co-operation with the representatives of the profession,
takes measures to regulate printing. Thanks to this intervention
by the church and thanks to the moderation of the interested
parties (whose professional rules are characterized by humanitar-
ianism and charity), Geneva avoids the strikes which, at that
time, trouble Lyons and Paris. This social peace contributes to
economic recovery and the booming of prosperity.

We can see that Calvin's contribution to the understanding of
the significance of salary is very important. While in the discussion concerning just salary, most theologians seek to establish a
norm by starting from a hypothetical natural law, Calvin exactly
places the problem in its biblical light by showing that salary
can be understood only when we consider the gratuitous remuneration of God who, through Jesus Christ, grants forgiveness and

life to men. The salary therefore cannot be determined only and first of all by an objective, quantitative criterion. It must first be seen in relation to the real needs of the workingmen considered in their new dignity as children of God. This does not forbid, but on the contrary, it commands the state to exercise a certain control over salaries. Salaries must be guaranteed by contractual regulations. Finally, in case of conflicts, one must recur to arbitrations.

3. Commerce as a Visible Sign of the Interdependence of the Creatures of God

The purpose of economic goods and human work is to serve society. God calls each man to a particular task and thereby makes him, for the other human activities, dependent on the work and services of others. The division of work is according to the purpose of God. It shows the interdependence of his creatures, called to live in society. It is the concrete, visible, and necessary expression of their solidarity. It implies a permanent exchange between individuals—a reciprocity which binds them one to another.

Commerce is the indispensable complement to the division of work. Exchanges are made necessary for the realization of the harmonious social order which God has prescribed. Material trade is the sign of spiritual communion of the members of society. The immediate goal of commerce, therefore, is to procure for each man whatever he needs in order to live. Commerce must relieve the pain of man and render his existence pleasant. In order to respond to the purpose of God, commerce always must tend to this goal.

When turned away from its divine purposes, commerce rapidly changes its nature. Fraud and dishonesty make economic relations practically impossible; they isolate men and groups and undermine the social order which is indispensable to exchanges and to life.

Dishonesty in business, therefore, is not only a fault against human morality; it is a sacrilege, inasmuch as it distorts the order of God from its purpose. Dishonesty in business is an offense against the goods and the services with which the Creator intends to benefit men for the support of their existence. "When men can no longer buy or sell," Calvin says, "human society is as shattered."

Contrariwise, evangelization by calling forth the birth of man to new life makes him apt to commercial service. From external submission to the law, which man defrauds as soon as possible, the Christian passes to willing obedience, to the ethics of liberty. The Christian thus finds again the condition of a normal exchange and contributes to the restoration of the economic order necessary to the life of all.

But as this regeneration is only partial in the present life on earth, as church and society never become one, and as Christians themselves remain sinners, an external order must regulate commercial and traffic operations. This is one of the tasks of the state. By all means the state must facilitate the fluidity of trade and the regularity of exchanges. By law it must especially protect the quality of the instruments of exchange—the contracts, weights, measures, and coins.

"In order to feed men in friendship and peace," says Calvin, "it is required that each man possess what is his, that there be sales and purchases, that heirs succeed to those whom they must, that donations take place, and that each man may become rich according to his industriousness, vigor, dexterity, or other means. In sum, government requires that each may enjoy what belongs to him."

"Nevertheless, if men seek to enrich themselves by evil and illicit means . . . that is like a falsification." And "if the weights and measures are false, there will no longer be trade; buying and selling will no longer be possible. Men will be like savage beasts among themselves. If coinage is not sound, all transactions will be like stealing and brigandism."

Speculation, cornering, and monopolizing are the principal forms of a vitiated economic order. These forms were particularly widespread and common in the sixteenth century when living costs rose from day to day and merchants stocked the goods most necessary for life in order to profit from rising prices. In such circumstances, with prophetic boldness, Calvin cleaved speculators asunder. Monopolists* are nothing less than murderers because they block the circulation of goods necessary for life. "Today when everything has such a high price," Calvin says, "we see men who keep their granaries closed; this is as if they cut the throat of poor people, when they thus reduce them to extreme hunger."

It is well known that the Reformation had immediately instituted in Geneva a certain price control for goods of first necessity: wine, bread, and meat. This control by the state, protecting an equitable distribution of common goods among all people and combating stocking, hoarding, speculation, and monopoly, was completely in line with the thought of Calvin.

Our Reformer is the first theologian who, with such clearness, discerned the providential role which trade exchanges and commerce play in society and in the preservation of humankind.

The Middle Ages, as well as Luther and the principal Reformers, held tradesmen and merchants in less esteem and reproached them with being the cause of increasing luxury, of rising living costs, and of simultaneously increasing the richness of some and the poverty of others.

Calvin has not failed to recognize certain dangers in business. He has not ignored its abuses and excesses. As his predecessors, he denounced them. Yet he never ceased emphasizing just as much the providential role of commerce and its intrinsic dignity.

Calvin's remarks about the honesty of contracts, measuring instruments, and commercial ethics, as well as his considerations about monopolies, are today verified by modern science. Without a minimum of honesty and of trust, trade is impossible, economic life is stagnant, and man's isolation destroys the realization of a community. We will briefly mention the almost unsolvable problems met today by men who are interested in the economic development of countries whose ethics rests on other foundations than Christian ethics. In such societies there are unsuspected inti-

---

* Translator's note: That is to say, stockers and hoarders.

mate relations between missionary work or evangelistic action
and the development of a social and economic life conformable
to God's purpose. And an inverse relation is also evident: the
extension and the development of a civilization whose economic
life is encroaching, monopolizing, and plundering, if connected
with Christian witnessing, contribute to render null and void
such a witnessing. Such a civilization indeed gives the lie to
Christian witnessing.

4. Money Commerce and Banking

It is assuredly with regard to the commerce of money that
the economic thought of Calvin proved to be the most perspica-
cious as well as the most revolutionary.

The reader undoubtedly recalls that Scholasticism (basing
itself on the theory of the intrinsic unproductivity of money
already worked out by Aristotle) called illicit the deduction of a
recompense on loaned money. The prohibition of loans at interest (already passed by the Council of Nicaea in 775 and several
times formulated anew by the church councils and popes) was
enforced by the church through the centuries.

This rule, however, permitted numerous exceptions. Loans
at interest had been admitted under the form of a limited joint-
stock company involving risks and indemnity. A lender, moreover, was authorized to claim from the borrower an indemnity
(under the name of *interesse*) when the loan caused him a real
damage. When this damage could be measured, it could be
compensated by an equivalent sum (under the title of *damnum
emergens*). The lender who deprived himself of a real gain (for
example, in missing the occasion of buying an object which he
could have resold at a profit) could exact a sum equal to the
missed gain (by reason of the *lucrum cessans*. Finally, if the loan
involved a foreseeable risk, the lender had also the right to ask
for an indemnity (due to the *periculum sortis*). These were as
many extrinsic titles to loaned money which could be advanced
in order legitimately to ask for an interest and which the princes
and teachers of the church admitted with greater or lesser tol-

erance, according to places and circumstances. The church did this so well that, in spite of canonical interdicts, the practice of remunerated interest was common and developed with increasing rapidity at the dawn of the sixteenth century.

The Spanish sovereigns Charles the Fifth and Philip the Second, though they were good Catholics, were the first to recognize that interest was legitimate on the condition that it did not pass 12%. Henry the Eighth did the same, and in 1545 he fixed the rate of interest at 10%.

In Geneva the loan at interest is practiced well before the Reformation. Recognized by the Franchises of Adhémar Fabri in 1387, loan at interest is protected by the Duke of Savoy who has no feeling of guilt in coining this protection into money. The rate of interest is quite variable. Generally money is lent between fairs* for three months at 5%, which is to say, 20% per annum.

Yet the canonical prohibition remained. In 1532 the University of Paris condemned the principle of remunerated loans.

At the beginning of the sixteenth century, the economic life of Geneva passes through a period of severe restrictions. The fairs are deserted; merchants and bankers abandon the place. The perturbations born of the war with Savoy are succeeded by the troubles of the Reformation. The minutes of notaries show that loans are very rare. In 1527 money is lent at 5%. But with the recovery of Genevese economic life, caused by the arrival and activity of Reformed refugees, the need of credit made itself felt anew. The law, which had set the legal rate at 5% in 1538 (before the definitive return of Calvin), still keeps it at this same level in 1544, then lets it rise to one per fifteen, that is, 6.6%. But the controls are strict, and, in fact, this legal authorization is, according to Calvin, to be a curb more than a stimulus for business in the city of Geneva. The reason is that Calvin has formulated a doctrine about lending money at interest. This doctrine was a revolution in the history of theology and a stimulus for economic life, yet it remained restrictive in many regards.

---

* Translator's note: Fairs were periodical gatherings, taking place every three months, for the sale of goods.

Our readers well know that in this matter the early Reformers remained faithful to medieval tradition. They condemned the receiving of interest for loans, yet admitted customary exceptions. Toward the end of his life, Luther came to consider as usury not the interest in itself, but rather too high a rate of interest.

Freed by his faith from all slavery to tradition, Calvin approaches the problem in an entirely new way. Calvin consults the Bible, yet at the same time, he carefully analyzes economic mechanisms in order to find out to which living reality he must apply the practical lessons of the Word of God. This analysis of our Reformer is a forerunner of the modern scientific method.

What does Calvin find in the Bible?

He finds first a realistic picture of a mankind generally given to profit seeking. For this reason, according to Calvin, the Bible condemns usury and all its abuses. The Bible, on the other hand, emphasizes with even greater force the value of loans without interest in view of helping our neighbor. Such a gratuitous lending is an authentic sign of faith. Hence the Bible rightly condemns receiving interest when the loan was given in view of relieving the needy.

Yet, is this biblical prohibition to be legitimately applied to all forms of loan at interest? Calvin sounds economic reality with an astonishing lucidity. He establishes that when the Bible speaks of interest or usury, it does not aim at all at the relatively new and widely spreading phenomenon called production loan. It is not a question here of giving aid to a person in danger or difficulty. Here one does not run the risk of taking advantage of the poverty of a man by having him pay for the loan made in his favor. Here it is a question of lending a sum in view of creating a working capital. Now, if I rent a landed property to a man who will exploit it, why could I not ask for a rent from him who uses my personal property (that is, my money) to exploit it? Calvin therefore rejects the centuries-old adage, notably expounded by Aristotle and Thomas Aquinas, which says that money does not produce money. Calvin affirms that on the contrary money is just as productive as any other merchandise. Let us therefore not apply to production loan the biblical teaching about consumption loan.

Moreover, Calvin adds, if we prohibit all usury, we reject the honest lenders along with those real usurers who profit from the misery of men.

Nevertheless, Calvin is constantly aware of the real status of humanity contaminated with sin. Hence Calvin does not fail to discern prophetically the abuses to which the loan at interest can lead us once that it is declared legitimate. Hence he fences this legitimation with all sorts of restrictions. Calvin's idea is to curb actively the aggressive power of money.

First he denounces as an act of avarice the act of investing for profit a sum of money which ought to be used for helping a person known to be in need. Further, it is illicit to receive interest from a poor man even when the law permits it. Moreover, interest must not be accepted if the borrower of a sum has not earned through the loan a sum equivalent to the interest. Finally, any interest beyond the legal rate is to be condemned.

But what is the normal rate of interest? In this as well as in other cases, Calvin refuses to set objective norms. The determining factor is the responsibility which the lender (inspired by the charity of Christ) takes for the borrower before God.

Since not all men are Christian and the Christians themselves remain sinners, the state must set relative norms in order to keep a certain order. In establishing this norm, the state must look not only at the private interests of the lender and the borrower. The state must also keep present the public interest. With an analytical mind which goes far beyond the economic science of his time, Calvin calls attention to the fact that the rate of interest has an effect upon living costs and that ultimately most of the interest is paid by the consumers.

It has been said, not without good reasons, that liberation from the prohibition of loans at interest constitutes a turning point in history. But we must emphasize the fact that in the spirit of our liberator Calvin, liberation did not mean total freedom for this practice. To Calvin's restrictions limiting and controlling this practice, his successors added reservations which well reveal their true sentiments. As the businessmen of Geneva planned founding a bank to facilitate the placement of their savings at a legal rate of 10% (although this was much lower than elsewhere), the ministers, headed by Théodore de Bèze, protested. "Riches are far from being desirable for Geneva," they said; "on the contrary, they would be pernicious. Riches would inevitably be followed by luxury, worldliness, love of pleasure, and an infinity of evils which would not be fitting to a republic whose reputation depends on the regularity of her mores."

As we can see, according to the thought of Calvin and the Genevese ministers, trafficking in money must be made easy in proportion as it is necessary to the development of industry and commerce. Yet, as all legitimate economic activity, it must be controlled and contained in sane limits. The reason is that social life must not be perturbed by all sorts of excesses to which sinful men give themselves once that they have been freed from all restraints.

5. Calvinism and Capitalism

Several sociologists like Max Weber and Ernst Troeltsch have tried to explain the extraordinary industrial development of Protestant societies by starting from various aspects of Calvin's doctrine.

These are in brief the theses of Weber:

Max Weber analyzes the sociological make-up of some industrial regions and notes that there are in proportion far more Reformed men devoted to commercial and financial techniques than the representatives of other confessions or religions.

It seems evident therefore, he says, that Reformed Protestants generate a certain spirit which facilitates the development of capitalism.

In what does this spirit (which Weber calls the capitalist spirit) consist? Weber notes that what moves capitalist activity is in no way the desire of enjoyment or of possession. The reason is that this desire has existed in all societies and at all times. The capitalist spirit consists in the desire of gain. What moreover characterizes the passage from a pre-capitalist situation (where as in all primitive societies each man works just enough to satisfy his vital needs) to a capitalist situation is that this desire for gain (and consequently the desire to work beyond the necessary minimum) becomes common to a whole population. Now, in order that such a character be stamped on a whole people, Weber continues, it must be connected with religion. Now, and more precisely, Calvinism is the first Christian ethics which gave a religious character to work. Before Calvinism, work was a part of the activities belonging to material life; a man had to work if, in one way or another, he could not dispense with work; but these secular activities had no relationship with eternal salvation and spiritual life.

In Calvinism, on the contrary, work is considered as a divine vocation, work becomes a religious activity. Man will, henceforth, work at all cost, even if he does not need to earn a living, because working is a command of God. And basing himself on the ethics of work which prevails in the Puritan societies of the eighteenth century, Weber illustrates this theory with striking examples taken especially from the writings of Benjamin Franklin.

Weber then asks why work is a religious act among Calvinists. And he answers, Because of the dogma of predestination. This dogma, says Weber, is most characteristic among the tenets of Reformed faith and gives a meaning to each act of the believer. First of all, it creates individualism. Each believer, in fact, trusting that his salvation is the object of an individual decree of God, acts with reference only to himself.

Moreover, this dogma of predestination has transformed medieval asceticism into an ethics of action. While the Catholic believes that he must work out his own salvation in avoiding contamination by the activities of this world, the Calvinist, on the contrary, thinks that his faith is verified and tested by secular activities. If he is not an elect, this fact will be shown in his work; but if he is an elect, all his activities will bear the mark of divine blessings. And the more he will be visibly blessed in his undertakings, the more certain will be his election. Now, this condition engenders two characteristics connected with the development of a capitalistic society: On the one hand, men are hard workers, but, on the other hand, out of contempt for earthly pleasures men spend very little. Seeking pleasure is indeed a sign of divine reprobation of men given to pleasure. The result of this working hard and spending little is saving; and this saving will be always in search of new investments. For Max Weber, Calvin has displaced the center of gravity of asceticism. The Middle Ages insisted on an asceticism away from the world; Calvin introduces an asceticism in the midst of the world.

Then, secularization of society came in; faith in predestination disappeared. But the asceticism in the world was maintained and transformed by Protestants into a secularized middle-class ethics which glorified work, saving, and profit at the expense of the major spiritual qualities. Such is, according to Max Weber, the origin of the ethics which underlies every capitalist society.

What are we to think of this theory?

First of all, we must note that Weber analyzes a capitalism which is quite different from its origins. The thought and ways of the Puritanism of the eighteenth century have been strongly influenced by religious and profane factors which were utterly alien to Calvin. Weber's analysis is accurate but is applied to a society which is later than original Calvinism. In other words, Weber's grave fault is to confuse a later form of Protestantism with the original Calvinism.

Weber is accurate, for example, in saying that predestination played a primary role in the Calvinism of the eighteenth century, but he is inaccurate in attributing to predestination a preponderant place in the mind of Calvin. It is only later in life that Calvin developed this doctrine of predestination, and he did so in reaction to certain attacks which he received.

Weber is also right in asserting that Puritan societies have extolled the virtue of work to a maximum and that this glorification of human work became greater as secularization progressed. Work truly became a god of our middle class. The current homage paid to a dead man which says, "Work was his life," is a typical characteristic of our bourgeois paganism.

This middle-class paganism was reached at the cost of ignoring everything that Calvin had said about work. What we have said about the duty of subjecting work to spiritual life through sanctification ought to be sufficient to show that capitalist ethics is the very opposite of the ethics found in the Gospels.

Weber finally is correct in saying that Puritan societies despised pleasure to the point of the most severe austerity thereby stimulating saving to excess. But we have shown that for Calvin austerity was imposed by the hard times which the early Reformed people had to undergo. Moreover Calvin never erected austerity into a virtue. Our Reformer never attributed any meritorious value to asceticism.

Concerning saving, we have previously and precisely noted that Calvin could be justly criticized for having missed seeing the role which saving plays in the economic development of any society. Calvin dreaded avarice and hoarding. Hence he insisted on the fact that accumulated economic goods ought to be put again into circulation in view of mutual help. Calvin cannot be blamed for the excessive concern for saving which in fact characterizes the Puritan industrial world of the eighteenth century.

It is clear that if Max Weber had studied the Calvinism of the sixteenth century and not that of the eighteenth century, he would have reached different conclusions. He would certainly have noted that early Calvinism carried in itself the virtues of an industrious society, but that it also reckoned with deviations in human nature and anticipated sufficient curbs to keep men from falling into the excesses of a society submitted to the priority of gain and enslaved to profit as the only rule of life.

The shift from Calvin's anthropology to an increasing secularized optimistic notion of man led certain Protestant societies to the deviations analyzed by Max Weber.

In order to conclude this argument, let us return to the Calvinism of Calvin.

The reader will note that, with respect to his Roman Catholic or Protestant predecessors, Calvin had a quite original economic thought. While practically all former theologians made economic life depend on a general and natural ethics which was in no direct relation with the work of redemption, Calvin was the first to show that material life is in reality one of the objective places where, with his concrete behavior, man inscribes and shows his faith in the redeeming Christ. It is so much so that economic relations among men (who are naturally vitiated by sin) can be restored by the spiritual renewal of the creature. Evangelization and mission therefore ought to have a direct effect on economic life. Both are a condition of the restoration of economic life in view of a harmonious social life.

It cannot be denied that Calvin's rehabilitation of economic life once despised by the church had considerable repercussions on the development of Protestant societies.

Yet Calvin is not responsible for the fact that his rehabilitation of work and money later degenerated into men's making work and money their gods. On the contrary, with an emphasis before him unknown, did not Calvin remind men that they ought to subject their money and work to God? Did he not proclaim the economic solidarity of men and nations, the necessity of a continuous redistribution of riches, and the legitimacy of the state's intervening to discipline economic life? If these principles had been respected, the evolution of capitalism would very probably have been quite different from what it came to be.

There is no doubt that Calvin's emphasis on personal responsibility would never have led him to ask the state to be the exclusive animator of economy. Yet Calvin's awareness of the ambiguity of man's nature (that is, of the plain fact that man is constantly solicited by both God and Mammon) would never have inclined Calvin to believe that society can reach a harmonious economic activity through the simple play of individual interests.

This is why it would be fitting to call Calvin's concept of economic life a "personalist socialism," or, if one prefers, a "social personalism." Calvin seeks an ever new equilibrium between safeguarding the rights and goods of the person, on one hand, and respecting the needs of society as a whole, on the other.

In conclusion, we shall quote this magnificent passage of Calvin which in a striking way sums up his economic and social thought—a thought which is equally concerned with the person and with society:

"We must begin with the goal which is to find out what emotion and intention the Lord wishes us to have toward earthly goods. What are the licit means to acquire them? What is their right and legitimate use?

"Our first point, therefore, is that we must not seek the goods of this world because we covet them. If we are in poverty, we must bear it patiently. If we have riches, we must put in them neither our love nor our trust. We must always be ready to give them up when God will think it good for us. Whether we have them or not, we must scorn them as ephemeral. We must prize the blessing of God as being more valuable than the entire world. We must seek the spiritual Kingdom of Christ without getting involved in evil desires.

"Our second point is that we must honestly work for a living; that we take the gain coming to us as bread from the hand of God. May we not use evil traffics to draw the goods of others to ourselves but rather serve our neighbor with a good conscience. May we accept the profit of our labor as a just salary. In selling and buying, may we use no fraud, no ruse, no lie. Let us go squarely to our task with the same faithfulness and loyalty which we require and expect from others. The last point means that he who has little ought not to fail to thank God and eat his bread with contentment, and he who has much ought not to misuse his wealth in gluttony or intemperance, in lavish expenditures or superfluous things, in pride or vanity; he ought to use his riches moderately for himself and employ the power which riches give him in aiding his neighbors and relieving them from suffering, acknowledging himself as receiving goods from God, on condition that he must eventually account for them. We always ought to think of Saint Paul's comparing the goods of this world to the manna: He who has a great quantity of it ought to eat some to his satisfaction and give the rest to him who has none. In brief, just as Jesus Christ gave himself to us, so by charity we ought to impart to others the graces which he gave us. Riches are a means to help the needy. That is the way to proceed and to keep a happy medium."

IV

CALVINISM AND OUR TIME

We must now come to the point. What can we keep of Calvin's social humanism which we have expounded? To what do the thought and wishes of Calvin (a man of the sixteenth century) lead us (men of the twentieth century)?

First of all we must make a remark:

1. Calvinism Is Out-of-Date

To say that Calvinism is outdated may in certain respects seem extremely presumptuous. God does not often give, to his church, men like Calvin who change the course of history and transform society on a large part of our earthly globe. A man may address to Calvin all the reproaches he wishes; any man may flatter himself with the illusion that he is more enlightened than Calvin; yet men cannot suppress the fact that this Reformer still marks, with the imprint of his faith and thought, millions of inhabitants of this planet. These millions are of course not aware of this fact. More evident is the fact that Calvin's influence on several Christian confessions is far from being spent. It is moreover quite possible that, after four centuries needed to appease Christian confessionalisms, only today, through some of his interpreters such as Karl Barth, is Calvin's teaching beginning to bring fruits in Christendom as a whole, in spite of antiquated confessional barriers.

In any case, only a man completely ignorant of what is now going on in Christendom can relegate Calvinism to the storehouse of outdated doctrines which have fallen into disuse.

The fact however remains that, on the basis of the teaching of

Calvin himself, Calvinism is outdated. The reason is that our Reformer did not intend to constitute a body of doctrines to remain valid for all times. His ambition was to understand all the aspects of the Word of God and to translate it most completely into the lives of men living in a definite period of history. And Calvin did this with the mentality of his contemporaries and in the precise circumstances of his time. Our faithfulness to Calvin therefore does not permit us merely and lazily to repeat mechanically his words in a new historical situation. It requires, on the contrary, that Christians make in their new circumstances the effort of submission to the Word of God in all things, following Calvin's magnificent example.

This was excellently expressed by Karl Barth when he said: "We accept Calvin as an example or as a model only in the measure in which he has, in an unforgettable way, pointed out to the church of his time the road of obedience: obedience of thought and deeds, social and political obedience. An authentic and true follower of Calvin has only one road to follow: obeying not Calvin himself but the one who was the Master of Calvin."

It is important, therefore, for us to discern in the action and teaching of Calvin what is perishable and what, on the contrary, remains valid today on condition of being actualized by an effort of creative imagination which keeps present the new circumstances in which we live.

In this sense we wish to note three ever actual aspects of Reformed thought. It is a question (a) of a complete humanism, (b) of an ecumenical humanism, and finally (c) of a universal humanism.

2. A Complete, Personalist, and Social Humanism

We live at a time when we are offered several humanisms which mutilate the human person of one of its dimensions.

We face first of all a wholly technical and scientific concept of man whose influence becomes every day more impressive. Made strong by fascinating scientific discoveries, this technical and scientific humanism tends to see the human creature only as an objective fact whose qualities are all measurable and numerable. Detached from the mystery which in God gives him life and originality, the human being becomes a laboratory abstraction which becomes every day drier and more hopeless.

On the other side, we face an equally atheistic humanism which further reduces man by its seeing him as being a compound of social factors.

On the one side, we have thus the scientific individualism of the West; and on the other, the collective humanism of the East.

In facing these two humanisms, our churches are paralyzed.

Toward scientific humanism, our churches have an inferiority complex. The powerful seduction which science exercises upon contemporary minds leads a great many Christians to deny that which constitutes the originality of biblical revelation. Ashamed of receiving the truth about man only from a Word of God, these Christians would at all costs reduce a divine Word to an experimental knowledge so as to give to it the semblance of science.

And in facing Communist humanism, our churches tremble with fear. Easily impressed by the subversive power of atheism, some of our churches lose confidence in the historical and universal sovereignty of their Lord. Overwhelmed by the misdeeds of collectivism, other churches have kept their trust in the sovereign action of the Christian revelation. The most orthodox on the doctrinal plane are set in a religious and political individualism which is totally forgetful of man's social dimensions so clearly taught by the Bible. The amputation of this social dimension of man leads many churches to an inversion into piety or to a liturgical introversion of compensation which reinforces their dramatic isolation from the masses and their aloofness from political problems.

We can at once see, in these circumstances, what fruits the humanism of Calvin can still bear for us.

Calvin's insistence in keeping parallel the knowledge of man derived from God and the knowledge of man derived from man invites us again to find a complete humanism, without mistrusting science yet without scorning biblical revelation; a humanism taking into account the person in its totality; a humanism made known by God's revelation, on one side, and by science, on the other.

Moreover, by his biblical vision of society, Calvin has preserved humanism from its individualistic vitiation. He has made evident the universality of our humanness.

Calvin opened and traced a pathway for a humanism which combines the knowledge of the person with a keen awareness of social realities.

The application, to our churches, of the biblical teaching on the circulation of goods ought to impel us to serious reflection and to upsetting reforms. The function of deaconship and the ministry of money at the service of our communities ought to be thought anew. The deacon is really a minister. His service is exactly on the same footing as the other ministries. Gathering gifts and using them wisely is not the only function of a deacon. The deacon is to raise in each member of the Christian community (be he rich or poor) the spiritual problem of his material life, of his goods, of his time, and of his capacities, in view of freely putting them at the service of God and neighbor. Pastors, deacons, and church members together are to rediscover an essential part of Christian discipline. At present this is really being done in several churches of Calvinist origin.

In certain communities the financial condition of the church members is examined; then a scale of gifts is proposed to each member. This scale of gifts varies according to the income and fortune of each member. Such Christian communities do not only consider the financial needs of the parish and church administration but also take in Protestant mutual aid, relief work, evangelization, and foreign missions.

In other Christian communities, five or six young people come freely together in view of submitting themselves to a new common discipline. This discipline takes in the exercise of their spiritual life, the use of their time, their work, their leisure, and the use of their money.

There are also groups of married couples and groups of single persons who periodically meet in order to compare their budgets, to help one another mutually, and to submit their decisions to a brotherly examination.

Incidentally, the teaching which Calvin drew from the Gospels concerning the circulation of wealth outside the church keeps all its actuality for the rest of society.

If we examine modern economic life by the light of this teaching, we shall find that science confirms the exactness of many observations of our Reformer Calvin. Prosperity becomes general when the benefits of riches are shared among all men, when the means of production are spread among all, and when the work of each person receives an equitable part of collective wealth.

But how many obstacles are set still against this general diffusion of riches and working tools! It is enough to mention the immense zones of pauperism which in our day persist in the world alongside the zones of accumulation—where economic goods (of which we are the beneficiaries) pile up.

The example of Calvin ought to lead us to renew continuously our political and social concepts by the Word of God and to confront them with the new realities of our time and world.

The social ethics of our Reformer is a dynamic ethics which forces the Christian to be always up-to-date in thought and action.

Nothing is more contrary to the spirit of Calvin than a conservative spirit.

The gospel exacts from Christians the unceasing quest of a complete humanism which takes into consideration the person in his totality and society as a whole.

In this sense, this humanism must be (from an ecclesiastical point of view) ecumenical.

3. An Ecumenical Humanism

When, for Calvin and the Reformers, it was a question of entering into the thick of the fights of the sixteenth-century conflicts, none of them had the idea of struggling for the purpose of preserving strictly religious or churchly truths or of salvaging a church. What made them enthusiastic was the idea of rediscovering in its entirety the truth about God and man. Their primary passion was to make that truth triumph over men. At all costs the Reformers wanted to free mankind from all its servitudes and particularly from its religious mystifications. It was only secondarily, and as if in spite of themselves, that the Reformers became the adversaries of the church as institution. And all the Reformers became truly anguished as they realized that a part of Christendom could not become aware of the illness which it suffered, and that the official church threw them out of her bosom. It was with death in their souls that they saw themselves compelled to constitute separated churches. And even when reduced to this extremity, they did not think for a minute (and Calvin less than any of them) that they were forming autonomous churches definitively cut off from the rest of Christendom.

On the contrary, the Reformers were conscious of belonging to the authentic church; to the newly rediscovered historical church; to the restored Christian church; to the apostolic church, holy and catholic as ever; to the only body of Christ. And the Reformers suffered at seeing the members of this body momentarily and externally divided among themselves.

Those men, who picture the Reformers as founders of a religious sect seeking to cultivate for itself an ideal religion, commit both a historical error and a theological error. None of the Reformers ever meant to found anything that would call itself Protestantism and would last for eternity. Calvinism was never willed or planned by Calvin. Historically, Calvinism is not a phenomenon by itself. It is simply an episode in the history of Christianity. And the history of Christianity is simply an aspect of universal history.

Nothing therefore is more alien to Calvin than the confessionalism which erects such-and-such a fraction of Christendom into a close and self-sufficient entity.

"We believe that no one should withdraw apart and be contented with his own person, but that all together must keep and support the unity of the church . . ."—says article 26 of the

La Rochelle Confession of Faith, composed by Calvin and adopted by the first national synod of the Reformed churches of France in 1559.

For Calvin, the church is one, not because Christians from anywhere must be united, but because they have unity already, through faith, as members of the body of Christ.

And, for our Reformer, the church is universal not only because there are believers scattered over the whole world, but because first of all the living Christ is the only Savior of all men on earth and all will appear before him at the end of history.

The human divisions of its members can do nothing against the fact of the unity of the body of Christ. These divisions are only accidental; and even though very serious, they are only superficial and provisory.

Calvin does not contest the fact that in the papal church still exist visible remnants of the church to which he is united. And all that Calvin can do to avoid a break, he will do as long as there is a hope of reconciliation.

He goes through Europe and he is present at all conferences where discussions with the Roman Church have some chance to succeed. He is at Hagenau in 1540, at Worms in 1541, and at Ratisbon. When excluded from the dialogue, he continues the conversation in writing by commenting upon the first decisions of the Council of Trent. He declares that he would gladly "let his head be cut off provided that peace be re-established in the church." And when there is no longer any hope coming from the Catholic side, he attempts the impossible in order to re-establish the unity of Protestantism which is divided in the Lutheran, Zwinglian, Anglican, and Reformed parties. Being aware of the diversity of human reactions to the Word of God, Calvin does not try to impose a compact and monolithic unity. He draws a distinction between "the teaching which builds up the church" common to all Christians and the diversity of interpretations and customs allowed to each denomination. "Do not make a chasuble* or a candle to be an obstacle or a difficulty," he says.

---

* Translator's note: This is a sleeveless vestment of a celebrant at Mass or Eucharist.

Invited in 1552 by Cranmer, the Anglican Archbishop of Canterbury, Calvin declares himself ready "to cross ten seas if necessary" in order to realize the unity of the church.

In order to serve this unity one must not give in on the plane of truth. On the contrary. Because it is only through rigorously proclaiming the only truth which is in Christ that the unity of Christians will visibly be realized. The more we will strip the gospel of the religious additions of paganism (always reborn in the heart of man)—additions such as superstitious rites, obscure liturgies, folkloric customs, local traditions, images, alien philosophies and doctrines—the more quickly we shall find ourselves again united in Christ.

Of all the Christian confessions, Calvinism is the most ecumenical because of this fundamental reason: Calvinism has never been enclosed in a rigid, absolute, and final definition of its tenets. Calvinism has always proclaimed that the only authority of the church is the Bible which witnesses to Christ who himself is the Word of God and the sovereign authority—the living authority to which the church is submitted. The church therefore never possesses a truth of her own. All the church can do is to let herself be led ever anew and be re-formed by this only truth which is the living Christ—the eternal Christ who by his Holy Spirit is active in human history.

The church therefore is always in movement, always becoming, always reformable, always in quest of new discoveries concerning the truth about herself.

The humanism of Calvin therefore has no religious boundaries; it is open to all mankind. It is a universal humanism. It breaks all barriers which men set up between themselves. For in Christ national, ideological, and racial boundaries are abolished.

4. A Universal Humanism

If Calvinism is ecumenical by nature, it is also such for a political reason. The clear distinction which Calvin made between church and state has everywhere avoided the confusion between religion and nation. It has put in evidence the universal character of the Christian faith.

The struggle which Calvin in Geneva led against the mystic patriotism of the nationalists is not an accident.

It is, on the contrary, the historical expression of the necessary and perpetual contrast between authentic Christian humanism and the various forms of religious nationalism.

Religious nationalism is that primitive mystic force born of the paganism which is by nature in the heart of every man. It deifies clan and tradition. It erects into a sacred virtue the magic fears of groups which threaten the clan. It extols and glorifies the enthusiasm for revenge. It exalts the military and warlike virtues which at one and the same time stimulate sacral terror and vindictive hatred; and it incorporates them in piety.

Religious nationalism is one of the permanent forms of corruption of humanity. It urges societies to set themselves one against another and to destroy themselves by war.

The Christian church (when she is faithful to the Christ who is the liberator from demons) is the only force which can combat this permanent scourge. Inasmuch as she is the community of the members of the body of Christ spread over the whole earth, the church is the only universal power which ought to be capable of disclosing, laying bare, and holding in check this malevolent manifestation of primitive paganism. The church ought to be the only efficacious protection of humanity.

When Christianity, however, ceases to be faith in the only Word of God, so as to become a natural religion, it lets itself be corrupted (as any other religion) by this mysticism of clan, of nation, and of army.*

Historically, the beginning of such a perversion of the Christian faith goes back to the time of Emperor Constantine.

For three centuries, Christianity had remained aware of its originality with regard to the various forms of natural religion and official mysticisms held in honor in the Roman Empire.

Christianity was constituted of an ensemble of spiritual communities which were rooted in different regional societies made clearly distinct by languages and customs yet remaining united

---

* Translator's note: Thus it becomes mere nativism.

in the communion of the only Savior. The universal character of the Christian faith was a decisive factor for the members of the primitive church. Their solidarity with the other human groups was subordinated to their quality as citizens of the unique Kingdom of Christ. And their submission to the conventional religious manifestations as well as their obedience to the demands of the state were clearly made conditional and limited by their subjection to their only Lord.

During three centuries of missionary conquests, during the expansion of Christianity through the nations, Christians refused to carry arms.

But starting from the moment when state and nation were considered Christian, a fundamental confusion installed itself in the hearts and in the minds.

After the early centuries, the history of the Christian church is in all domains a history of assimilation (on the part of Christianity) of religious customs and mores alien to the faith found in the Gospels and issuing from Christ.

The worship of the nation, of forefathers, and of local and later national traditions little by little associated itself with Christian worship and encrusted it.

Allegiance to the order of this world came to be confused with the loyalty due to Jesus Christ. It was so much so that aggressive or defensive armaments and wars came to be considered as religious actions. And military heroism (once glorified by paganism) came to be added to the virtues extolled by the church. Then theology came in consciously to prop, to strengthen, and to justify these assimilations and identifications. Theologians got busy erecting huge doctrinal structures about patriotism and war. These doctrines lasted for a long time because they were made to rest upon biblical data. These data (that is, quotations from the Bible) were really fragmentary and fragile, yet theologians gave them extension and emphasis.

The Reformation did not escape this confusion. The Reformation was born at the beginning of the rise and development of European nationalisms. In certain respects the Reformation expressed these nationalisms. The Reformers were absorbed by

so many religious problems placed on the level of conscious reflection, that they were unable to discern all the problems surging
below this level. In this domain they did not let the Word of God
pierce through natural (or native) religion and immediately free
men from so many taboos.

It is thus that the reforms of Luther, of Zwingli, and of the
Anglican reformation were closely mixed up with typically nationalistic movements.

These various reformations kept a regional character which
imposed upon them well-defined political and geographical lim-
itations.

But this did not happen to Calvin's Reformation.

In Geneva, the Reformation was favored at its beginning by
a strong nationalistic current. Had it not been for the spiritual
energy of Calvin, Genevese nationalism would have absorbed the
Reformation.

But by rigorously and uncompromisingly affirming the sole
authority of the Scriptures in all the domains of life and by
emphasizing Christ's unique Lordship over church as well as over
society and state, Calvin by one stroke put an end to the national
myth and unveiled the dark spiritual power which makes the
nation sacred.

In his implacable struggle against the faction of those who
called themselves patriots, Calvin pointed out, with no possible
misunderstanding, the proper and correct place which state
authority and patriotism should have in the life of the Christian.

Calvin denounced the falsely religious character of nationalism. He unmasked its pretentions and tendency to fuse itself with
the Christian faith and to use the church to its own ends.

It is certainly this stand of Calvin which permitted Calvinism
to spread rapidly in all lands and among all peoples.

Wherever Calvinism was introduced, in Europe and in America, then in Africa and Asia, being marked by no national character, it installed itself with a feeling of independence and made
explicit the universality of the church of Christ.

But this Reformed universalism in course of centuries became weaker. It disappeared in proportion to the way that Christians (abandoning the Word of God) lost their awareness of their quality of members of the one cosmic body of Christ. The Reformed communities became diluted in the midst of a nation to the point of confusing themselves with the national environment.

And, in modern Protestantism as well as in Catholicism, natural religion having gone ahead of faith in the Word of God, the mysticism of the nation re-entered the church. Thus "national" churches came to be spoken of—a thing which would have been unthinkable at the time of Calvin.

The Christian churches in the world, therefore, no longer offer all the resistance with which they ought to oppose all the various forms of natural religion, the dark forces of primitive paganism, and, in particular, the destructive power of nativism and nationalism.

These dark powers are today more active and more pernicious than ever. Under the various aspects of sabre-rattling nationalism, of fanatic nativism, of bragging militarism, of segregating racialism, these obscure and destructive forces are reborn here and there and a little everywhere.

They upset or subvert the peoples of Africa and Asia. In the East they set one nation against the other. And in developed continents, where the concept of nation is dilated to the limits of civilization, ideologies take the place of nationalism and bring all the primitive mystic forces of clan religion to a focus.

Ideology is the modern lay form of natural paganism. It is a profane mysticism, a secularized form of human religiosity produced by the rational and atheistic scientific mentality of our technical age. Ideology has the power to raise up a sacred enthusiasm, to set human groups one against another, and to lead them finally into destruction.

In such a situation we can well see what Calvin can still offer to the world. Calvin's universal humanism can save us from corruption and destruction.

Calvin's evangelical teaching about state-church relations ought to be taken again under consideration and applied to the realities of today.

Trusting the unique Savior of the world, Christians ought to give the example of firm, objective, positive, and constructive patriotism. Their civics ought to be stripped of all ideological mystifications. Christians ought to contribute actively to demythologize the state, the nation, and the army. Christians ought to remind the men of today that political authorities and military institutions have a purely technical and profane task to perform. Neither state nor army is able to create, to safeguard, or to maintain what confused people call spiritual values. Only Christ generates such values. Through the universal action of the church, his work should actively go on above and through all political, ideological, and religious boundaries.

The state's mission is to provide a wholly human and temporal order. In the exercise of the profane function which is proper to government, the state is an authority established by God. As such the state must be respected, whatever may be the political regime on which the state rests.

If the state, however, claims for itself an ideological mission, it must be firmly contradicted on this point whatever the state dispositions toward the church may be.

The reason is that history shows that when the political authority puts on a religious or ideological character which flatters the natural paganism of the people, the state (with the mighty means of propaganda at its disposal) may lead the most enthusiastic peoples to the worst catastrophes.

The psychological means and services at the disposal of modern armies at present constitute one of the greatest dangers which threaten the human race. Christians ought to be particularly severe toward these powerful organs which are ever ready and inclined to change themselves into offices of ideological propaganda.

Concerning the army and its preparation for war, Christians in this matter ought also to reconsider altogether their position.

Here also, though it is stained with certain characteristics of his time, the thought of Calvin is still able to guide the thought of the Christian church.

We have said that the position of Calvin concerning the use of arms was full of caution.

With the Reformer Zwingli, Calvin vigorously denounced the militarism of the partisans of military service.

Calvin proclaimed the idea that Christianity ought to be defended with arms as being quite contrary to the Christian faith.

Yet, against the Anabaptists who rejected any participation in war, Calvin asserted again the traditional justification of armies which is founded on chapter 13 of Paul's Letter to the Romans. According to this doctrine, military action is licit when it is undertaken by the legitimate authority to protect the geographical territory on which it exercises its power.

It is fitting to add, however, that Calvin has stated precisely that according to the Scriptures, even in lawful war, means which annihilate populations or hurt nature are forbidden. "God bridles the license to make damages in the midst of war ardor," he writes. This is why "though the law of war opens the door to plunder, pillage, and excesses, yet as far as possible one ought to guard himself that the soil be not spoiled and disfigured to the point of being made barren for the future. In brief, when a man has to fight and get the spoil of his enemies, he ought not to lose view of the utilities of the humankind."

The massive means of destruction at the disposal of modern armies ought to force serious Christians to ask two questions from the Scriptures; no believer claiming to acknowledge the Reformed principle of the only authority of the Word of God can avoid them.

The first of these two questions is the following: According to Calvin's method of understanding Scripture, can we still purely and simply apply the passage of chapter 13 of the Letter to the Romans (which justifies political authorities' carrying the sword) to the military enterprises and means of modern states? In spite of a seemingly common principle, are we not in fact facing two objective realities which have no common standard?

And now the second question: Are the present-day means of destruction (atomic or non-atomic) still compatible with the mission which Paul assigns to the state which uses the sword?

Considering what Scripture tells us about creation, about men, and about nature, and keeping present the expositions which Calvin gave of them, it is very difficult to pretend that our Reformer has given an affirmative answer to those two questions.

We must ask ourselves whether or not it is God himself (who by the menace of the total and radical destruction of humanity represented by modern preparations to war) who invites his church completely to revise her position regarding the use of arms, to repent, and to acknowledge that the traditional theological justification of war (which the church once believed itself able to give) is in no way according to the Gospels. In history there have been opportunistic interpretations of Scripture which, once facing the facts, reveal themselves as indefensible. Christendom has known this *a posteriori* (this is, in Latin, "from what comes after") justifications of customs and mores which are simply collective aberrations, and yet people won't give up. Did not theologians, for example, justify slavery? Has not the Scripture been used to justify anti-Semitism and racialism?

We are here simply raising these questions without pretending to be able to answer them immediately.

It does not seem rash, however, to affirm that Christianity will be unable to make progress in the immense masses of other continents, to render the service which it is called to render to the men of our time, and to victoriously face the world of tomorrow if Christianity does not give an entirely new answer to these three essential problems: money, armies, and Christian unity.

What had made the Reformation a success was the boldness with which (starting from Scripture) it criticized the most sacred traditions and ways of its time, and the ardor with which it sought (in the face of new circumstances) a more just application of the teachings of the Word of God.

Instead of locking ourselves in the easy habit of only lazily repeating the ancient formulae, Calvin's example ought to urge us to make an ever new effort to renew our faithfulness and to bring our thinking up to the level and circumstances of our time.

It belongs to the heirs and followers of the Reformation to ask essential questions today and evermore answer them according to the teaching of Sacred Scripture, without worrying about conformity to current opinion. Such is the most important contribution which Reformed people (who are faithful to their divine call and who remain in the continuity of their history) can at present make to their country and then to Christendom as a whole, and such is the most important service finally which they can render to humanity.

BY THE SAME AUTHOR

LA PENSÉE ÉCONOMIQUE ET SOCIALE DE CALVIN
(The Economic and Social Thought of Calvin)

Preface by Antony Babel

Geneva: Georg & Cie, 2nd ed. 1961

LITURGIE ET ARCHITECTURE, le temple des chrétiens
(Liturgy and Architecture, The Christian Temple)

A sketch of the relation between the theology of worship and the architectural conception of the Christian churches, from their beginnings until our day.

With a notice from Karl Barth: "The problem of the architecture of the places of worship in Protestantism."

45 original sketches by R. Schaffert

Geneva: Labor et Fides, 1961

L'HOMME ET LA FEMME DANS LA MORALE CALVINISTE
(The Man and the Woman in the Calvinistic Morality)

The Reformed doctrine on love, marriage, celibacy, divorce, adultery, and prostitution is considered in its historic framework.

Preface by Madeleine Barot

Geneva: Labor et Fides, 1963